MW00795706

THE TYPOGRAPHIC DESK REFERENCE

Theodore Rosendorf

The Typographic Desk Reference TDR

Foreword by Ellen Lupton

Oak Knoll Press

First Edition 2009
Third Printing

Copyright © 2009 Theodore Rosendorf

ISBN 978-1-58456-231-3

Published by
Oak Knoll Press
310 Delaware Street
New Castle, DE 19720 USA
www.oakknoll.com

Publishing Director & Copy-editor:
Laura R. Williams

Designed by Theodore Rosendorf.
The principal text is set in Adobe Caslon
by Carol Twombly (with additional
custom glyphs by Theodore Rosendorf).

♾ Printed by Sheridan Books, Ann
Arbor, Michigan, on acid-free paper
meeting the requirements of ANSI/NISO
z39.48–1992 (*Permanence of Paper*)

Library of Congress Cataloguing-in-
Publication data available from the
publisher

For Darci

Contents

Foreword

A foreword is a short commentary placed at the front of a book. Typically, it is written by someone whose reputation is believed to cast a flattering light on the work to follow. A foreword thus provides a note of introduction that is more social in character than summative or substantive.

The author of this foreword offers a courteous welcome to both the readers and the writer of the book to follow. "Hello, my friends," she says. "It is my pleasure to share with you the work of my friend and colleague Theodore Rosendorf, a young man who has devoted himself wholly and without regret to a typographic life. I share with him this modest yet admirable calling. Together, we have suppressed our own worldly desires and ambitions in order to allow the written word to sit with comfort and grace upon the printed page. You, our readers, may also share this simple calling. You will discover on the leaves that follow an account of typographic terminology that has been rigorously edited and thoughtfully designed. You will find no other book that quite duplicates the purpose of this one, and certainly you will find none that has been prepared with so much intensity and devotion. These pages reveal an admiration for typography's long history as well as an awareness of its current concerns and anticipated evolution. A book such as this belongs on the shelf of anyone who works in the service of typography."

The word "forward" is sometimes mistaken for "foreword." Make not this error, but do move ahead to encounter the wisdom that is stocked so plentifully on the pages that lie just beyond this one.

Ellen Lupton

Acknowledgements

Along with family, friends, and colleagues, grateful acknowledgement is made to the following for their guidance and support: ATypI, John D. Berry, Brad Blanar, Thierry Blancpain, Valentin Bruŝtaux, Matthew Carter, Ricardo Cordoba, Dave Crossland, Tim Daly, Simon Daniels, Viĉtor Gaultney, John L. Gornall, Dr Shelley Gruendler, Ted Harrison, William Heerman, John Hudson, Barbara Jarzyna, Robin Kinross, Stefán Kjartansson, Ellen Lupton, Michael Mitchell, Mark Parker Miller, Hrant H. Papazian, Lorenza Pavesi, Oliver Perrin, Thomas Phinney, Albert-Jan Pool, Dan Reynolds, Nick Rosendorf, Erik Spiekermann, Eric Stevens, Kon T., Tiffany Wardle de Sousa, Frank N. White, Susan Wightman, and Laura R. Williams.

Introduction

Usually placed after a foreword, preface, or acknowledgement, an introduction states the nature or purpose of the text that follows. A substantial introduction written by someone other than the author is typically grouped with the front matter and paginated with Roman numerals. Otherwise, it's placed at the beginning of the text and paginated with Arabic numerals—like this introduction—starting on page 1.

While pagination serves to associate it with the front matter or main text, the introduction floats somewhat free in order to serve its purpose. Similarly, this book is positioned somewhere between quick reference and in-depth analysis.

I wrote the *Typographic Desk Reference* (TDR) to answer an industry need. For all of the wonderful books available on type, none are solely devoted to quick reference across the entire craft. As a launching point for more comprehensive inquiry, the TDR doesn't exhaust each particular subject; it's instead a bridge from the desk to the arsenal of volumes we turn to for inspiration and insight.

Because typography is a vast subject, I've limited the TDR to Latin-based writing systems, with emphasis on form and practical application. Mention of software and printing technology has been kept to the essential minimum. The same goes for discussion of hand-set metal type, except in cases where modern terminology finds its roots in that endangered art.

Most importantly, this book belongs to its readers. Feedback received will directly affect subsequent editions. Please feel free to get in touch with your suggestions or observations through talk@typedeskref.com.

Theodore Rosendorf

Terms

A series Based on the ISO 216 standard, sizes of paper having a $1{:}\sqrt{2}$ aspect ratio. It begins with an A0 size sheet measuring 1 m² or 841 × 1189 mm. Successive sheets in the series (A1, A2, A3, A4, A5, etc.) are sized by halving the preceding paper size parallel to its shorter side. Below are the sizes in millimeters. *See also* B series, C series, DIN, ISO.

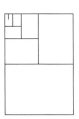

A0	841 × 1189	A3	297 × 420	A6	105 × 148	A9	37 × 52
A1	594 × 841	A4	210 × 297	A7	74 × 105	A10	26 × 37
A2	420 × 594	A5	148 × 210	A8	52 × 74		

across the gutter Elements of a layout that extend across the spread, spanning the gutter margin. Also called *gutter jump*. *See also* gutter, gutter margin, spread.

agate / ruby Invented by George Bruce in 1822, a 5.5 pt printing type used for tabular data in newspapers. At a little over 13 lines to an inch, it was considered the smallest point size to be reliably printed on newsprint, though now there are even smaller faces. Also called *agate line* and *column inch*. *See also* type size.

alignment The setting of text in relation to its margins. Text can be aligned one of four ways. *Justified:* aligned on both the left and right margins. *Ranged left:* (*flush left*, FL, or *ragged right*) aligned to the left margin with the right ragged. *Ranged right:* (*flush right*, FR, or *ragged left*) the opposite of ranged left. *Centred:* symmetrically set on a central axis. *See also* margin.

alphabet A set of abstract symbols contained within a particular writing system. *See also* GLYPHS.

alphabet length   The width of the entire alphabet of a given typeface at a certain size, used to calculate copyfitting. *See also* alphabet, copyfitting.

alphanumeric   Consisting of or using both letters and numerals. A character that exists both as a letter and a number.

ANSI   American National Standards Institute, headquartered in Washington, DC. The organization coordinates US standards with international standards. ANSI is the US's ISO member body. *See also* DIN, ISO, NISO.

ASCII   American Standard Code for Information Interchange. A universal format for representing and exchanging alphanumeric characters between separate systems. ASCII defines base glyph information, absent of formatting or style. It is based on the English alphabet and defines character codes for 128 characters: 95 printable and 33 non-printing. *See also* Unicode.

ATypI   The Association Typographique Internationale. A not-for-profit organisation democratically run by an elected board, ATypI is a global forum for the type community and business. Its administration is based in the USA and the organization holds a conference in a different world city each year. *See also* ATypI-Vox.

ATypI-Vox   A type classification system invented by Max-imilien Vox in 1954, and adopted in 1962 by the Association Typographique Internationale. The system contains eleven groups, each based on general characteristics of form often typical of one century. The groups are *Humanist, Garalde, Realist, Didone, Mechanical, Linear, Inscriptional, Script, Hand, Blackletter,* and a general *Non-Latin* group. Some of the categories can be further grouped into Classicals (*humanists, garaldes, and realists*), Moderns (*lineals, didones, and mechanicals*), and Calligraphics (*inscriptionals, scripts, and hands*). *See also* page 97.

auto-kerning Algorithmic calculations that compare kerning pairs and glyph outlines to automatically apply kerning. *See also* kern, kerning, kerning pair.

auto-tracing The software conversion of bitmap images into bézier outlines. *See also* bitmap font, bézier splines.

B series Based on the ISO 216 standard, a geometric mean between an A series sheet of the same number and the A sheet with the next number down (B1 is a geometric mean between A1 and A0). The sides of B0 sheets are 1 m to $\sqrt{2}$ m. Successive sheets in the series (B1, B2, B3, B4, B5, etc.) are sized by halving the preceding paper size parallel to its shorter side. Below are the sizes in millimeters. *See also* A series, C series, DIN, ISO.

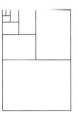

B0	1000 × 1414	B3	353 × 500	B6	125 × 176	B9	44 × 62
B1	707 × 1000	B4	250 × 353	B7	88 × 125	B10	31 × 44
B2	500 × 707	B5	176 × 250	B8	62 × 88		

back up To align baselines on opposite sides of a printed sheet. *See also* baseline grid; ANATOMY & FORM: baseline.

bad break An incorrectly hyphenated word or a line or page break that causes the text to not make sense. *See also* break, orphan, widow.

banner The logotype design of the name of a publication, such as a newspaper, newsletter, or magazine usually appearing at the top of the page. Also called *flag*. *See also* logotype.

base align To arrange type on a common baseline across columns. *See also* baseline grid, column; ANATOMY & FORM: baseline.

base to base The vertical measurement of type from baseline to baseline. Also written *b/b, B/B, bb,* or *B to B*. *See also* leading; ANATOMY & FORM: baseline, leading.

base
base

baseline grid A grid spanning across a layout, spaced in relation to the baseline measurements of its primary body text. *See also* ANATOMY & FORM: baseline.

bearoff To correct justification by adjusting the spacing between letters. *See also* justification, letterspacing, kern, spacing.

begin even To set the first line of a paragraph flush left, or full out, on the margin and not indented. *See also* margin, paragraph; ANATOMY & FORM: flush paragraph, indent, outdent.

berliner A newspaper sheet size measuring about 470 mm × 315 mm (18.5″×12.4″). Also called *midi*. *See also* broadsheet, tabloid.

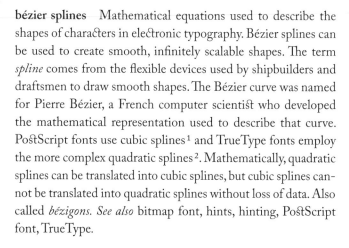

1   2

bézier splines Mathematical equations used to describe the shapes of characters in electronic typography. Bézier splines can be used to create smooth, infinitely scalable shapes. The term *spline* comes from the flexible devices used by shipbuilders and draftsmen to draw smooth shapes. The Bézier curve was named for Pierre Bézier, a French computer scientist who developed the mathematical representation used to describe that curve. PostScript fonts use cubic splines[1] and TrueType fonts employ the more complex quadratic splines[2]. Mathematically, quadratic splines can be translated into cubic splines, but cubic splines cannot be translated into quadratic splines without loss of data. Also called *bézigons*. *See also* bitmap font, hints, hinting, PostScript font, TrueType.

bicameral Two alphabets joined together. The Latin alphabet is an example of a bicameral alphabet, as it has an uppercase and lowercase. *See also* unicameral; ANATOMY & FORM: lowercase, uppercase.

bidirectional font A font with the technical ability of being set in both left-to-right and right-to-left directions.

bitmap font A font which is made up of pixels (*square dots*). Bit-maps are at a set size and cannot be scaled beyond their original size. Bitmap fonts typically work in tandem with outline fonts (*bézier splines*), with bitmap fonts being used for the on-screen display of the original outline font. Also known as *screen font*. *See also* bézier splines, hints, hinting, PostScript font, TrueType.

bleed   Text or graphics that extend beyond the edge of the page. After printing on an oversized sheet, the bleed is trimmed off.

blind folio   A page within a count of pages, but lacking a page number. *See also* folio.

body copy / type   The main textual content set in one face and point size, with a common leading and column width. Also called *body copy/matter, book face/font,* and *text. See also* column, copy.

bottom margin   The margin at the bottom of a page. Also called *foot margin* or *tail margin. See also* margin.

bottom of text   The position of the last line of text at the bottom of a page of typical length. Folios and running feet are spaced in relation to this last line of text. *See also* bottom of type page, folio, footer/running foot.

bottom of type page   The position of the element appearing at the lowest point on the page. This could be the last line of text, a foot folio, or a running foot. *See also* bottom of text, folio, footer/running foot.

bouncing folio   A folio (page number) with varied position in relation to the last line of text on a page. Also called *bounce. See also* folio.

boustrophedon   Alternating lines written in opposite directions; one line is written from left to right, then the next line's letters are reversed, and written from right to left. Its name comes from the Greek word βουστροφηδόν (*ox-turning*). Boustrophedon writing was used in ancient Safaitic scripts and pre-historic and archaic Greek inscriptions.

Left to Right
Right to Left

break The point where type is divided. This may be the end of a line or paragraph, or as it reads best in display type. *See also* bad break, paragraph.

broadsheet A newspaper sheet size measuring 74.9 cm × 59.7 cm (29.5″ × 23.5″) per spread. The broadsheet format is twice the size of a standard tabloid. Australian and New Zealand broadsheets use an A1 paper size (84.1 cm × 59.4 cm). *See also* A series, berliner, tabloid.

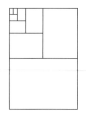

C series Used for envelopes, the C series are measurements based on the ISO 269 standard. C series sizes are a geometric mean between A and B series sheets of the same number (C1 is a geometric mean between A1 and B1). An A4 sheet will fit into a C4 envelope, an A4 sheet folded to A5 will fit into a C5 envelope, etc. Below are the sizes in millimeters. *See also* A series, B series; DIN; and ISO.

C0	917 × 1297	C3	324 × 458	C6	114 × 162	C9	40 × 57
C1	648 × 917	C4	229 × 324	C7	81 × 114	C10	28 × 40
C2	458 × 648	C5	162 × 229	C8	57 × 81		

California job case A later version of the typecase used to sort hand-set lead type. Within the drawers, the type is arranged based on the frequency of use. *See also* lowercase, uppercase.

calligraphic Originating from the Greek word *kalligraphia*, meaning *beautiful writing*, roman or italic alphabets appearing to have been written with a pen or brush. *See also* CLASSIFICATION & SPECIMENS: Calligraphic.

callout An excerpt of text set prominently away from the body type to provide emphasis. Also called *block quotation, blurb,* and *extract. See also* body type.

camera-ready copy / CRC A document that is ready for reproduction. Also called *mechanical, composite art,* or *paste-up. See also* offset lithography printing.

caps and lowercase   Type set in capitals and lowercase or the instruction to do so. To set text in Latin, Greek, or Cyrillic alphabets. Also called *Clc, C/lc, C&lc, Ulc, U/lc,* and *U&lc. See also* bicameral; ANATOMY & FORM: capitals, lowercase.

caps and small caps   Type set in capitals and small capitals or the instruction to do so. Also called *caps and smalls, Csc, C/sc,* and *C&sc. See also* ANATOMY & FORM: capitals, small capitals.

caption   Text describing a photo or graphic. Captions are typically written in the present tense. Also called *cutline, underline,* or *legend.*

castoff   The number of pages a manuscript will make based on a character count. *See also* character count, copyfitting.

chapter head   A heading for titling chapters. *See also* heading.

character   An abstract symbol. A letter, punctuation mark, or figure. Traditionally called *sorts. See also* GLYPHS.

a€?3

character count   The number of characters in a selection of type or a manuscript. *See also* castoff, copyfitting.

character set   A single font's collection of characters, symbols, and numbers. *See also* GLYPHS.

characters per pica /cpp   A measure of the amount of characters of a particular font that will fit within one pica. Used for copyfitting. *See also* character count, cicero, copyfitting, pica.

chase   A rectangular frame used to secure sorts (*metal type*) into position in letterpress printing. *See also* composing stick, letterpress printing, sort.

cicero   A Continental European typographic measurement, where 1 cicero equals 12 Didot points, or 4.51 mm. *See also* Didot point, pica, type size.

cold composition   The setting of type with mechanical *golf ball* or *daisy wheel* typewriters. Also referred to as *strike-on composition* or *impact printing*. *See also* daisy wheel, golf ball.

colophon   A page at the back of a publication defining the book's creation. A colophon can include facts about its production, artists, designers, or printers, and may specify typefaces and papers used. Also a printer's mark or emblem. The word originates from the Greek word κολοφών, meaning *summit*. *See also* the last printed page of this book.

column   A taller than wide block of text occupying a copy area. *See also* column balancing.

column balancing   To set multiple columns of type to have equal height. Typically used when type is set on a spread of less than three columns. *See also* column, copyfitting, justification.

composing   The process of setting type. Setting metal type is referred to as *hand composition*. Also called *comp*. *See also* chase, composing stick, letterpress printing, sort, typesetting.

compositor   A person who sets type. *See also* composing.

composing stick   A device used to set lines of metal type, which are then bound into a chase (*frame*) for printing. *See also* chase, letterpress printing, sort.

copy   All typeset words and/or text incorporated into a publication. *See also* body copy/type.

copyfitting   To fit an amount of type within a specified space. *See also* castoff, character count.

creep   During the book binding process, when multiple sheets are folded at the spine, the fold's inner pages and margins extend or *creep* further out than the outer pages. A professional printer will account for these variances. Also known as *push out, thrust, feathering, outpush,* and *binder's creep. See also* imposition, signature.

crosshead   A running head centered on the measure over body type. *See also* body type, header/running head, heading, sidehead.

daisy wheel   A system for cold composition typesetting with typewriters, where raised metal type is positioned on spokes around a wheel that turns, positioning and striking each letter into the paper. *See also* cold composition, golf ball.

Didot point   A unit of typographic measurement used in Europe (except Britain), where 1 Didot point is equal to 0.3759 mm. 12 Didot points are equal to 1 cicero. *See also* cicero, point, type size.

DIN   Deutsches Institut für Normung e.V. (*The German Institute for Standardization*) is the German organization for standardization and its country's ISO member body. DIN 476—equivalent to ISO 216—defines A and B series paper sizes. DIN 678 (ISO 269) defines C series envelope sizes. As defined in DIN EN ISO 3098, DIN 16 and 17 (now defunct), and DIN 1451 contain definitions for several standard typefaces intended for use in technical product documentation and traffic signage respectively. DIN 16518 is a type classification system based on the ATypI-Vox system wherein each group is based on general characteristics of form often typical of one century. *See also* A series, ANSI, ATypI-Vox, B series, C series, ISO; CLASSIFICATION & SPECIMENS: DIN 1451, FF DIN.

dots per inch   The measure of resolution for print output. Not to be confused with *pixels per inch* (PPI). Also called DPI. *See also* pixels per inch.

drop folio   A folio (*page number*) dropped to the foot of a page when elsewhere it is set at the top of the page. *See also* folio, footer/running foot.

ductus   The combined elements of speed, angle, pressure, and type of pen used to form a letter.

àbç AQ 123

elite   A fixed pitch typewriter style typeface with a pitch of 12 characters per inch. *See also* pitch, fixed pitch.

end even   When text is justified, a last line of text ending at its right margin. *See also* begin even, justification, margin.

erosion   The thinning or disappearance of thin strokes in letter forms during output.

exception dictionary   A database of hyphenated words that a computer can use to automatically apply end of line rules for hyphenation. *See also* hyphenation & justification.

Fixed

fixed pitch   Monospaced type, where each letter occupies equal horizontal space. *See also* letterspacing, pitch, proportional spacing.

flex   The automatic suppression of small details such as cupped serifs in letters produced at small sizes. *See also* ANATOMY & FORM: serif.

flush   Opposite of ragged, the even alignment of text lines at a margin. *See also* alignment, ragged, ranged left, ranged right.

font   Derived from the word *found* as in type *foundry,* a font is a single representation of a typeface style, such as Times New Roman Italic. Also called *fount. See also* type family, type style, typeface.

folio   A page number. A folio may be set as part of a running head or foot, or in the outside margin. *See also* blind folio, bouncing folio, drop folio, footer/running foot, header/running head, margin.

footer / running foot   Containing folios and section titles, running feet are consistently positioned at the bottom of every page in a document. They're either aligned flush left or right (*inside or outside margin*), or centered to the measure of the main text. *See also* folio, header/running head, measure.

footnote   A note at the bottom of a page associated with a location and reference mark within the main text. *See also* GLYPHS: asterisk, dagger, double dagger.

fore-edge margin   The margin at the outer edge of a page of a book, opposite the spine. Also called *outside margin, or thumb margin. See also* gutter margin, margin.

foundry   A company that designs, produces, and distributes type. Traditionally, *foundry type* refers to hand set metal type.

full on the body   Type set with leading equal to the size of the type, as in type set at 10 point with 10 point leading. Also called *set solid. See also* leading, pica point.

full on the body 10/10

full word wrap   To set text without the use of hyphenation. *See also* hyphenate, hyphenless justification.

galley   In traditional typesetting, a proof of the running text, tables, or figures, before these parts are combined to form pages.

get in   To fit copy into less space than was initially estimated. *See also* castoff, copyfitting.

glyph   A shape used to represent a character or symbol within a writing system. *See also* GLYPHS.

glyph scaling   The process of slightly stretching or compressing glyphs when justifying text. Also called *stretching. See also* justification, justification engine, kerning, letterspacing, tracking, word spacing.

scaling
scaling
scaling

golf ball   A system for cold composition typesetting with typewriters. A ball the size of a golf ball, with letters molded on its surface, rotates and strikes each letter into the paper. *See also* cold composition, daisy wheel.

greeking   The use of gray bars or *dummy* characters to represent text that is too small to be legible when displayed on the screen. Also, the use of classical Latin text (*Lorem ipsum*) in a layout so that the design of the document will be emphasized rather than its content. Lorem ipsum, a passage from classical Latin literature from 45 BC, has been in use since the 1500s. The standard lorem ipsum text begins:

> *Lorem ipsum dolor sit amet, consectetur adipisicing elit, sed do eiusmod tempor incididunt ut labore et dolore magna aliqua. Ut enim ad minim veniam, quis nostrud exercitation ullamco laboris nisi ut aliquip ex ea commodo consequat. Duis aute irure dolor in reprehenderit in voluptate velit esse cillum dolore eu fugiat nulla pariatur. Excepteur sint occaecat cupidatat non proident, sunt in culpa qui officia deserunt mollit anim id est laborum.*

grid   A graphical layout for the design of pages of a book or other document. Variations on pages must match divisions in the grid.

Gutenberg, Johannes   Thought to be the independent inventor of movable type in Europe at the middle of the fifteenth century. *See also* movable type.

Gutenberg: unit of measure   A unit of linear measure equal to $\frac{1}{7200}$ inch, or about $\frac{1}{100}$ of a pica point. *See also* Didot point, pica point.

gutter   The space between two columns of type. Also short for *gutter margin*. Also called *alley,* or *column gutter. See also* column, gutter margin, margin, spacing.

gutter margin   The margin at the inside, or binding edge of a book. Also called *back* or *bind margin. See also* fore-edge margin, gutter, margin.

half title A page containing only the title of the book, set before the title page. Also called *bastard title.*

head margin The margin at the top of a page. Also called *top margin. See also* margin.

header / running head Section headings and/or subheadings repeated at the top of every page. *See also* crosshead, footer, heading, measure, sidehead; GLYPHS: en, em.

heading A title that introduces sections of text, usually set off by differences in size or position. In typesetting terms, multiple levels of heads and subheads are defined as A-head, B-head, C-head, etc. *See also* header/running head, subhead.

headline The large title of a news article or press release.

hell box A receptacle for broken or discarded metal type (*sorts*). *See also* letterpress printing, sort.

hints The definitions within an outline font that are referenced for hinting. *See also* bitmap font, hinting, bézier splines.

hinting The computed process of converting characters from outline to bitmap format for display purposes. Also called *grid fitting. See also* bitmap font, hints, bézier splines.

historiated letter A decorative initial cap typically containing hand drawn illustrations pertaining to the text that it begins. Also called *entrelac initial. See also* ANATOMY & FORM: versal.

hyphenate To split a word across lines, as an aid to uniform line breaking. *See also* hyphen, justification.

hyphenation zone The area at the end of a left aligned text line where it is acceptable to hyphenate words. *See also* hyphenate.

hyphenation & justification / H&J   To set text as hyphenated and justified. *See also* hyphenate, justification.

hyphenless justification   To set text as justified without the use of hyphenation. *See also* full word wrap, hyphenate, justification.

FRONT

BACK

imposition   The arrangement of page impressions on a printed sheet, folded to form a signature. Single or stacked signatures, when bound and trimmed, form a book. *See also* creep, signature, work and turn / work and tumble.

in pendentive   A style of typesetting where successive lines are indented until one word occupies the last line. *See also* indent.

interpolation   The mathematical method of creating missing data from the averages of neighboring elements. Used to create additional weights when designing type.

interword space   The horizontal space between words on a line. Interword space can be adjusted to achieve justification. *See also* justification, spacing; GLYPHS: space.

IPA   The International Phonetic Association, or its phonetic alphabet used by linguists and speech scientists. Used to define the sounds of spoken language, one symbol exists for each sound. *See also* GLYPHS: IPA.

ISO   International Organization for Standardization, headquartered in Geneva, Switzerland. Founded on 23 February 1947, the agency implements international cooperation on industrial and scientific standards. ISO 216—based on the German DIN 476 standard—defines A and B series paper sizes. ISO 269 (DIN 678) defines C series envelope sizes. ISO 217 defines untrimmed raw paper sizes RA (*raw format A*) and SRA (*supplementary raw format A*), intended to be trimmed down after printing and binding to match the A format. Though similar to the A series sizes, the RA and SRA dimensions are rounded to the full centimeter. Standards for Latin character encoding include ISO 646, 2022, and 8859. General requirements for technical product documentation are contained in DIN EN ISO 3098, wherein certain typefaces are defined—notably DIN 1451, and Isonorm. *See also* A series, ANSI, B series, C series, DIN, Unicode.

jumpline   An indication at the end or start of a continued article defining what page the article is continued on or from.

justification   The process of setting text to align to both the left and right margins. Spaces and/or characters are stretched or compressed to create even amounts of spacing within all of the lines of the text. Also called *full out*. *See also* alignment, glyph scaling, justification engine, letterspacing, margin, wordspacing; GLYPHS: space, tracking.

justification engine   A software algorithm used to justify text by incorporating letterspacing, wordspacing, and glyph scaling. Settings can be adjusted for entire paragraphs or line by line. *See also* alignment, glyph scaling, justification, letterspacing, paragraph, wordspacing.

kern   To adjust the space between individual pairs of characters. Not to be confused with letterspacing or tracking, which affects entire blocks of text. *See also* kerning, letterspacing, mortise, tracking; ANATOMY & FORM: kern, sidebearing.

kerning   The adjusted space between letters. *See also* kern, kerning pair, kerning table, letterspacing, tracking; ANATOMY & FORM: body, sidebearing.

kerning pair   Letter combinations used to define optimal space between characters within a font. *See also* kern, kerning, kerning table, letterspacing, tracking.

kerning table   A calculation table containing the horizontal spacing values—measured in fractions of an em—for glyphs in a font. *See also* kerning, kerning pair, letterspacing, metrics, tracking, width table; GLYPHS: em.

Latin The most widely used writing system in the world. The Latin alphabet—also known as the Roman alphabet—was derived from the Greek alphabet and developed by the ancient Romans to write the Latin language. During the Middle Ages its use spread to the Romance languages, Germanic, Celtic, some Slavic languages, and then most European languages. Christian proselytism eventually spread the alphabet's use to Amerindian, Indigenous Australian, Austronesian, Vietnamese, Malay, and Indonesian.

leading The adjustable vertical space between lines of type. *See also* ANATOMY & FORM: leading.

letterpress printing The printing of text with movable metal type. The type is inked and then pressed into a surface to obtain an image in reverse. The direct impression of inked media such as zinc plates or woodblocks onto a receptive surface. *See also* chase, cold composition, composing stick, movable type, offset lithography printing, photocomposition, sort, type.

letterspacing The adjustable space between letters of a word. *See also* fixed pitch, kerning, pitch, spacing, tracking, word spacing; GLYPHS: space.

letterfit The quality of spacing around characters. Also called *fitting*. *See also* glyph scaling, justification, letterspacing, tracking, word spacing.

line gauge A straightedge rule, marked with typographic units, used to measure typographic elements. *See also* cicero, Gutenberg: unit of measure, pica.

Linotype machine Invented in 1884 by Ottmar Mergenthaler of Baltimore, the Linotype machine produced single lines of cast metal type (*slug*) for printing. It was first used at the New York Tribune in 1886. The Intertype machine, with Linotype compatible matrices, was later developed in 1914. *See also* cold composition, letterpress printing, Monotype machine, offset lithography printing, photocomposition, slug.

logotype   Originating from the Greek word λογότυπος (*logotipos*), a corporate brand's trademark name set in a unique typeface. *See also* GLYPHS: monogram, registered trademark, trademark.

MATĂDOR°

lowercase   Originally, the small letters of metal type stored in the lower part of a printer's typecase. Modern use of the term refers to a font's small letters. *See also* California job case, uppercase; ANATOMY & FORM: lowercase.

ABC abc

margin   The area between columns of text or from the edge of the paper to the boundary of the layout area of the page. *See also* bottom margin, column, fore-edge margin, gutter, gutter margin, head margin.

matrix   A mould for casting lead type (*sorts*) used in letterpress printing. Also called *mat*. *See also* letterpress printing, punch, punchcutting, sort, type, type casting.

measure   The length of a line of typeset text. Also called *line length*. *See also* cicero, pica.

metrics   Font information such as ascent, descent, leading, character widths, and kerning pairs. *See also* kerning pairs, leading, width table; ANATOMY & FORM: ascent, body, descent, leading.

Monotype machine   A competitor to Linotype, the Monotype machine was patented by Tolbert Lanston in 1887 and put into production in 1897. As an advantage over Linotype machines, it made each character separately before assembling them into lines. Kerning was possible and further adjustments could be made after the type was set—essential for setting mathematical and scientific texts. *See also* cold composition, letterpress printing, Linotype machine, offset lithography printing, photocomposition.

mortise   An antiquated term for *kern*, originating from the practice of shaving metal type to decrease space between letters. *See also* kern, spacing.

movable type   A system of printing using movable pieces of type. Movable type was invented between 1041 and 1048 in China by Bi Sheng (畢昇) using baked clay and wood. In 1298, Wang Zhen (王禎) re-invented a method of making movable wooden type and later used wood carvings to cast sorts in copper, bronze, iron, and tin. In Korea, the transition from wood to metal type occurred around 1230 by Choe Yun-ui (상정예문). Thought to be an independent invention of movable type in Europe, the use of casting type based on a matrix and hand mould was introduced by Johannes Gutenberg in the middle of the fifteenth century. *See also* letterpress printing, sort.

Multiple Master   A PostScript Type 1 font format with the feature of continuous adjustment along axes of size, weight, width, extender length, terminal shape, and serif form. Multiple Masters can provide optical balance for type set at various sizes. *See also* PostScript font, TrueType.

mump   Derived from the old Dutch term *mompen* (to cheat), to mump is to pirate fonts.

NISO   National Information Standards Organization. The US organization that develops and maintains technical standards related to bibliographic and library applications. NISO is designated by the American National Standards Institute (ANSI) to represent US interests to the International Organization for Standardization's (ISO) Technical Committee 46. *See also* ANSI, DIN, ISO.

oblong   When a page is turned 90° to the right from its normal reading orientation. Also called *broadside*.

offset lithography printing   A printing technique where an inked image is transferred from a plate to a rubber blanket, and then to the printing surface. The lithographic process is based on the repulsion of oil and water. As ink is applied to the image area, an ink-repelling film of water is applied to the non-printing areas. *See also* cold composition, letterpress printing, photocomposition.

OpenType Created by Microsoft and Adobe Systems, a font format able to hold thousands of characters and alternate styles. An OpenType font can be either PostScript or TrueType. *See also* Multiple Master, PostScript font, TrueType.

optical adjustment The adjustment of kerning or tracking beyond a font's set metrics. *See also* kerning, tracking.

optical compensation To make visual adjustments to type set at sizes not intended for its design.

orphan An undesirable single line of a paragraph ending at the top of a page or column. Also called *club line. See also* column, widow.

orthography Derived from the Greek words ορθο ortho (*correct*) and γραφος graphos (*that writes*), orthography is a set of spelling, punctuation, and capitalization rules used in a writing system.

paragraph A block of text representing one idea, separated by a line break, indent, or outdent. *See also* begin even, end even, in pendentive; ANATOMY & FORM: box indent, elevated cap, flush paragraph, indent, outdent, versal; GLYPHS: pilcrow.

photocomposition A photographic process of typesetting where columns of type are projected onto photographic paper and in turn made into plates for offset printing. Also called *photo type setting* or *photosetting. See also* cold composition, letterpress printing, offset lithography printing .

Pi font A font containing mathematical or scientific symbols.

pica　A unit of typographic measurement used in the US. A pica consists of 12 pica points. 12 pica points = 1 pica; 6 picas = 1 inch; 72 pica points = 1 inch. *See also* cicero, Gutenberg: unit of measure, pica point, type size.

pitch　The amount of horizontal space occupied by a single fixed-width character. *See also* characters per pica, fixed pitch.

pixels per inch　The measure of resolution for screen or video input and output devices. Also called *PPI*. *See also* dots per inch.

point　The small unit of typographic measurement, and a subdivision of its larger pica or cicero. 1 *pica point* is equal to $\frac{1}{12}$ pica or $\frac{1}{72}$ inch. 1 *Didot point* is equal to $\frac{1}{12}$ cicero or 0.3759 mm. *See also* Didot point, Gutenberg: unit of measure, pica, type size.

PostScript font　First developed by Adobe Systems in 1976, fonts consisting of scalable outlines described with cubic bezier curves. *See also* bézier splines, bitmap font, Multiple Master, OpenType, TrueType.

abc mimi
ABC MIMI
abc mimi
ABC MIMI

proportional spacing　Type spacing where characters take up varying amounts of space. For instance, an i would take less space than an m. Also called *differential spacing*. *See also* fixed pitch, kerning, letterspacing.

proof　To read and mark manuscripts for errors and corrections. Also a document ready for evaluation. *See also* proofreader; GLYPHS: proofreaders' marks.

proofreader　Someone who checks a manuscript for errors and recommends corrections. Also known as *copyeditor*. *See also* proof; GLYPHS: proofreaders' marks.

punch　A tool used to impress matrices (moulds) that are in turn used to cast sorts (*individual pieces of metal type*) for use in letterpress printing. *See also* letterpress printing, matrix, punchcutting, sort, type, type casting.

punchcutting   The practice of cutting letter punches for use in type casting. *See also* letterpress printing, matrix, punch, sort, type, type casting.

ragged   Opposite of flush, the uneven alignment of text lines near a margin. *See also* alignment, flush, ranged left, ranged right.

ranged left   Text set aligned left and ragged right. *See also* alignment, flush, ragged, ranged right.

ranged right   Text set aligned right and ragged left. *See also* alignment, flush, ragged, ranged left.

recto   The right-hand, odd-numbered pages of a book or folded sheet. *See also* verso.

river   An unsightly vertical gap of white appearing to run down and through a paragraph of text. *See also* paragraph.

set   Contraction of typesetting. To set type. Also, the width of an individual character. *See also* pitch, typesetting.

side sorts   Infrequently used metal type stored to the side of a printer's typecase. *See also* lowercase, sort, uppercase.

sidehead   A heading set flush left or right over text. *Left sideheads* are aligned left, flush or indented. Usually for main headings, *Right sideheads* are set flush right. Right sideheads (or *shoulderheads*) are set in the outside margin at the top of the page. *Run-in sideheads* are set on the first line of type, separated with an en or em from the start of the text. *See also* crosshead, header/running head, heading.

signature   Two or more sheets of a book, connected at the binding. Sheets produced during the process of imposition. *See also* creep, imposition.

slug   A line of type cast as a single piece of metal on a linotype machine. *See also* linotype machine.

sort A single piece of metal type. *See also* chase, composing ſtick, letterpress printing, matrix, movable type, punch, punchcutting, type, type caſting, *Parts of a caſt metal sort,* page 84.

spacing The amount of space between words, letters, and lines within text. Many forms of spacing exiſt for setting text. *See also* fixed pitch, kerning, leading, letterspacing, tracking, word spacing; GLYPHS: space.

specimen A printed sample of type. See also *William Caslon's 1734 specimen,* page 98.

spread The left (*verso*) and right (*reƈto*) combined facing pages. *See also* reƈto, verso.

ſtyle sheet The definition of all type ſtyles and formatting rules used in a document.

subhead A heading following under a main heading. *See also* header/running head, heading.

tabloid A newspaper format measuring roughly 430 mm × 280 mm (17″× 11″) per spread, about half the size of a broadsheet. Also called *compaƈt,* or *kompakt. See also* berliner, broadsheet.

tabular setting Text set in the form of a table where each column is typically juſtified. *See also* column, juſtification.

text face A typeface designed for text or body copy. Also called *text letter* or *text type. See also* type size.

tracking The adjuſtable space between groups of letters. *See also* kerning, letterfitting, spacing; GLYPHS: space.

TrueType Developed in the 1980s by Apple and later adopted by Microsoft, fonts consiſting of scalable outlines described with quadratic bezier curves. *See also* bézier splines, bitmap font, OpenType, PoſtScript font.

type Printed or video/screen-rendered characters. A metal block containing a raised glyph on one end used to produce a printed impression of the glyph when inked and pressed onto paper. *See also* letterpress printing, matrix, punch, punchcutting, sort, type casting.

type casting To pour molten metal (typically an alloy of lead, antimony, and tin) into a bronze mould (*matrix*) to create sorts (*individual pieces of metal type*) for use in letterpress printing. *See also* letterpress printing, matrix, punch, punchcutting, sort, type.

type family A set of typeface designs with similar characteristics, but variations in style. *See also* font, typeface, type style.

type size The measure of a type's height in points. Beginning in the 17th century, a loose system of names existed to categorize sizes of type. The system became increasingly standardized by the 19th century, but was eventually abandoned in favor of standard numerical measuring systems. The names (English/American) with their averaged sizes in points are listed below. *See also* cicero, pica; ANATOMY & FORM: appearing size.

3	Minikin/Excelsior	18	Great Primer
4	Brilliant	20	Paragon
4.5	Diamond	22	Double Pica/
5	Pearl		Double Small Pica
5.5	Ruby/Agate	24	2-line Pica/Double Pica
6	Nonpareil	28	2-line English/Double
6.8	Emerald		English
7	Minion	36	2-line Great Primer/
8	Brevier		Double Great Primer
9	Bourgeois	40	Double Paragon
10	Long Primer	44	2-line Double Pica/
11	Small Pica		Meridian
12	Pica	43.2	Trafalgar
14	English	48	Canon or 4-line
15	2-line Brevier/Columbian		

type style   Variations of style within a typeface. Regular, bold, and italic, are the typical styles found in most faces. *See also* font, typeface; ANATOMY & FORM: bold, condensed, demi, expanded, italic.

typeface   A single variation or style of form. The term typeface refers to the design of a type family, meaning its style and shape that make it distinct. *See also* font, type family.

typesetting   The process of arranging type, whatever the means. *See also* chase, composing stick, letterpress printing, typography, sort.

typography   From the Greek words τύπος (*typos*) meaning *form* and γραφία (*grapho*) for *write,* the practice of creating, selecting and arranging or setting type. *See also* typesetting.

U&lc   Type set upper and lower case or the instruction to do so. *See* caps and lowercase.

unicameral   An alphabet containing one case, as with Arabic and Hebrew. *See also* bicameral.

Unicode   A character encodings standard, first published by the Unicode Consortium in 1991, to organize letters and symbols of all the world's writing systems. The current implementation of Unicode (version 5.0.0) contains over 1 million positions: 101,203 defined characters, 137,468 for private (custom) use, and 875,441 for future expansion. The code points consist of base glyph information, absent of format or style. *See also* ASCII, ISO.

unit system   A system of measurement with relative unit values equal to a fraction of an em within any set type. With a unit system, an equal amount of units will exist in type set at any size. *See also* GLYPHS: em.

abc ABC   uppercase   Originally, the large capital letters of metal type stored in the upper part of a printer's typecase. Modern use of the term refers to a font's capital letters. *See also* California job case, lowercase; ANATOMY & FORM: capitals.

verso   The left-hand, even-numbered pages of a book or folded sheet. *See also* recto.

widow   A single line of a paragraph's beginning at the bottom of a page or column. Also called *club line. See also* column, orphan, paragraph.

width table   A table of a font's individual glyph widths, measured in fractions of an em. *See also* kerning table, metrics; GLYPHS: em.

word spacing   The addition or subtraction of space between words. Fixed word spacing refers to text with equal amounts of space between words when text is set ragged. *See also* alignment, fixed pitch, kerning, letterspacing, ragged, spacing, tracking; GLYPHS: space.

word wrap   When a word in a line of text automatically breaks to the next line as it approaches its set column measure or the right-hand margin of the text block. *See also* column, margin, measure.

work and turn / work and tumble   The method of printing two copies of a document using one impression. One side is printed, the sheet is turned (side to side) or tumbled (end-over-end), then the other side is printed using the same impression. The finished sheet produces two copies. *See also* imposition.

Glyphs

Included in the entries are standard ISO and extended Latin characters, symbols, and diacritics. Unicode code points are defined in [square brackets] where applicable. For more on Unicode and ISO, see TERMS. All entries are alphabetized.

a-acute Inflected Latin letter *a* used in Czech, Ekoti, Faroese, Icelandic, Portuguese, Spanish, Welsh, and Yoruba. *See also* acute. [U+00E1, U+00C1]   á Á

a-acute-ogonek Inflected Latin letter *a* used in Navajo and Western Apache. *See also* acute, ogonek. [U+0105+0301, U+0104+0301]   ą́ Ą́

a-acute-underscore Inflected Latin letter *a* used in Kwakwala. *See also* acute, underscore. [U+00E1+0331, U+00C1+0331]   á̱ Á̱

a-arch (inverted breve) Inflected Latin letter *a* used in Serbo-Croatian poetics. *See also* arch. [U+0203, U+0202]   ȃ Ȃ

a-breve / short a Inflected Latin letter *a* used in Latin, Romanian, and Vietnamese. *See also* breve. [U+0103, U+0102]   ă Ă

a-breve-acute Inflected Latin letter *a* used in Vietnamese. *See also* breve, acute. [U+1EAF, U+1EAE]   ắ Ắ

a-breve-grave Inflected Latin letter *a* used in Vietnamese. *See also* breve, grave. [U+1EB1, U+1EB0]   ằ Ằ

a-breve-hoi / a with breve and hook above Inflected Latin letter *a* used in Vietnamese. *See also* breve, hoi. [U+1EB3, U+1EB2]   ẳ Ẳ ẵ Ẵ **a-breve-tilde** Inflected Latin letter *a* used in Vietnamese. *See also* breve, tilde. [U+1EB5, U+1EB4]

ặ Ặ **a-breve-underdot** Inflected Latin letter *a* used in Vietnamese. *See also* breve, underdot. [U+1EB7, U+1EB6]

ǎ Ǎ **a-caron / a-wedge** Inflected Latin letter *a* used in romanized Mandarin. *See also* caron. [U+01CE, U+01CD]

â Â **a-circumflex** Inflected Latin letter *a* used in Cree, French, and Welsh. *See also* circumflex. [U+00E2, U+00C2]

ấ Ấ **a-circumflex-acute** Inflected Latin letter *a* used in Vietnamese. *See also* circumflex, acute. [U+1EA5, U+1EA4]

ầ Ầ **a-circumflex-grave** Inflected Latin letter *a* used in Vietnamese. *See also* circumflex, grave. [U+1EA7, U+1EA6]

ẩ Ẩ **a-circumflex-hoi / a with circumflex and hook above** Inflected Latin letter *a* used in Vietnamese. *See also* circumflex, hoi. [U+1EA9, U+1EA8]

ẫ Ẫ **a-circumflex-tilde** Inflected Latin letter *a* used in Vietnamese. *See also* circumflex, tilde. [U+1EAB, U+1EAA]

ậ Ậ **a-circumflex-underdot** Inflected Latin letter *a* used in Vietnamese. *See also* circumflex, underdot. [U+1EAD, U+1EAC]

ȁ Ȁ **a-double grave** Inflected Latin letter *a* used in Serbo-Croatian poetics. *See also* double grave. [U+0201, U+0200]

à À **a-grave** Inflected Latin letter *a* used in Dogrib, French, and Italian. *See also* grave. [U+00E0, U+00C0]

ą̀ Ą̀ **a-grave-ogonek** Inflected Latin letter *a* used in Dogrib, Gwichin, and Sekani. *See also* grave, ogonek. [U+0105+0300, U+0104+0300]

a-hoi / a with hook above   Inflected Latin letter *a* used in Vietnamese. *See also* hoi. [U+1EA3, U+1EA2]

ả   Ả

a-macron / long a   Inflected Latin letter *a* used in Cornish, Latvian, and Maori. *See also* macron. [U+0101, U+0100]

ā   Ā

a-ogonek / tailed a   Inflected Latin letter *a* used in Polish, Lithuanian, and Navajo. *See also* ogonek. [U+0105, U+0104]

ą   Ą

a-ring / round a   Inflected Latin letter *a* used in Arikara, Cheyenne, and Swedish. Capital *Å* denotes the ångström unit of length in physics (10^4 Å = 1 μm). *See also* ring. [U+00E5, U+00C5]

å   Å

a-tilde   Inflected Latin letter *a* used in Portuguese and Vietnamese. *See also* tilde. [U+00E3, U+00C3]

ã   Ã

a-umlaut / a-diaeresis   Inflected Latin letter *a* used in Dutch, Dinka, English, Estonian, Finnish, German, Norwegian, Sami, Slovak, Slovene, and Swedish. *See also* diaeresis/umlaut. [U+00E4, U+00C4]

ä   Ä

a-umlaut-acute   Inflected Latin letter *a* used in Tutchone. *See also* acute, diaeresis/umlaut. [U+00E4+0301, U+00C4+0301]

ä́   Ä́

a-umlaut-grave   Inflected Latin letter *a* used in Tutchone. *See also* diaeresis/umlaut, grave. [U+00E4+0300, U+00C4+0300]

ä̀   Ä̀

a-umlaut-macron   Inflected Latin letter *a* used in Tutchone. *See also* diaeresis/umlaut, macron. [U+01DF, U+01DE]

ǟ   Ǟ

a-underdot / a-nặng   Inflected Latin letter *a* used in Twi and Vietnamese. *See also* underdot. [U+1EA1, U+1EA0]

ạ   Ạ

a-underscore   Inflected Latin letter *a* used in Kwakwala and Tsimshian. *See also* underscore. [U+0061+0331, U+0041+0331]

a̱   A̱

acute   A diacritic first appearing in Hungarian (á é í ó ú) in the 16th century. It is used to express lengthening of vowels (á é í ó ú ý)

é

in Czech and consonants (ŕĺ) in Slovak. It softens consonants (ćńŕśź) in Basque, Croatian, Polish (called *kreska* and with a more upright design), and romanized Sanskrit. In romanized Chinese it is used with vowels and one nasal (áéíńóúü). All vowels can appear with acute in Icelandic and Portuguese, and old Icelandic contains the ǽ vowel. It indicates stress in Spanish, and in Vietnamese, the acute is used to specify a rising tone. Athapaskan uses the acute for high nasal vowels (ą́ę́į́ǫ́ų́). The acute can also be found in Bosnian, Catalan, Danish, Dutch, Faroese, French, Gaelic, Italian, Lingala, Navajo, Norwegian, Occitan, Swedish, and Walloon. *See also* diacritical mark. [U+0301]

æ Æ   **aesc / æsc**   Pronounced *ash,* a ligature used in Faroese and Icelandic, and Danish, Norwegian, and Anglo-Saxon, where it typically represents the Swedish *ä*. In English, it represents the Greek αι (alpha iota). Its lowercase form appears in the IPA alphabet, representing a near-open front unrounded vowel. *See also* IPA. [U+04D5, U+04D4]

ǽ Ǽ   **aesc-acute**   Inflected Latin letter æ used in linguistics and old Icelandic. *See also* acute. [U+01FD, U+01FC]

ǣ Ǣ   **aesc-macron / long aesc**   Inflected Latin letter æ used in Anglo-Saxon and old Norse. *See also* macron. [U+01E3, U+01E2]

ɛ Ɛ   **African epsilon**   Additional Latin letter used in Dinka, Ewe, and Twi. The lowercase form is used in the IPA alphabet to represent a open-mid front unrounded vowel. *See also* IPA. [U+025B, U+0190]

ɛ̈ Ɛ̈   **African epsilon umlaut**   Inflected Latin letter Ɛ used in Dinka. *See also* diaeresis/umlaut. [U+025B+0308, U+0190+0308]

ɛ̃ Ɛ̃   **African epsilon tilde**   Inflected Latin letter Ɛ used in Kpelle and Twi. *See also* tilde. [U+025B+0303, U+0190+0303]

ɣ Ɣ   **African gamma**   Additional Latin letter used in Ewe, Kpelle, and in the IPA alphabet to represent a voiced velar fricative. *See also* IPA. [U+0263, U+0194]

ampersand Derived from the shorthand of Marcus Tullius Tiro in the first century AD and adopted for wide use in the first printing types of the 1460s, the ampersand is a ligature of the Latin word *et*, the sign (*&* & *&*) standing for *and*, as in Smith & Co. Also called *short and*. *See also* ANATOMY & FORM: ligature. [U+0026]

&

analphabetics Accessory symbols in an alphabet not considered part of the alphabet's fixed order. *See also* diacritical mark, punctuation marks.

~{(.*^´

angle brackets Angle brackets are used in mathematics for algebraic formulas and in classical texts for editing to mark additions. Not to be confused with greater than (>) or less than (<). *See also* braces, guillemets, parentheses, punctuation marks, square brackets. [U+2329, U+232A]

⟨a⟩

apostrophe Used to indicate either possession (Bob's book, boys' coat) or the omission of letters or numbers (don't, she's, class of '99), and in forming plurals with single (never more) letters (A's, B's, t's). A closely spaced version is used for consonants in Czech (d' and t', capitalized Ď and Ť) and Slovak (l' and L'). In some languages it represents a glottal stop. Also called *raised comma* or *single close-quote*. *See also* caron, comma above, dumb quotes, glottal stop, punctuation marks, quotation marks. [U+02BC, U+0313, U+0315, U+2019]

'
a

arithmetical signs The basic signs (+ - ± ÷ < = > ×) are included in most fonts, but the extended characters (≠ ≈ ≤ ≥ √ ∞) may not be. Note, the multiplication symbol (×) should not be confused with the letter x. [U+002B, U+2212, U+00B1, U+00D7, U+00F7, U+003C, U+003D, U+003E, …]

× ± ÷
< ≈ >

arch A diacritic used in Cyrillic and Serbo-Croatian (â ê î ô û r̂), mainly for linguistics. Also called *cap, dome,* and *inverted breve.* *See also* breve, diacritical mark. [U+0311]

â

asterisk Resembling an image of a star (*Latin astrum*), the asterisk was historically used in European typography to sym-

*
a

GLYPHS

bolize birth dates (the dagger, to symbolize the year of death). The asterisk appears in Sumerian pictographs and has been in use for at least 5000 years. Today, it is commonly used to mark footnotes. *See also* asterism, dagger, punctuation marks; TERMS: footnote. [U+002A]

asterism   Three asterisks placed in a triangle used to call attention to a separate sub-chapter. *See also* asterisk, punctuation marks. [U+2042]

at   Derived from the Latin preposition *ad,* at is a symbolic abbreviation for the word *at.* Giorgio Stabile, a professor of history in Rome, claims to have traced the symbol back to the Italian Renaissance in a Venetian mercantile document signed by Francesco Lapi on May 4, 1536. The document mentions the price of an @ (an amphora vase) of wine in Peru. [U+0340]

b-overdot / dotted b   Inflected Latin letter *b* used in old Gaelic. *See also* overdot. [U+1E03, U+1E02]

hooktop b   Additional Latin letter *b* used in Fulfulde, Hausa, and Kpelle. The lowercase form is used in the IPA alphabet to represent a voiced bilabial implosive. *See also* IPA. [U+0253, U+0181]

backslash   Aside from being used for computer programming, the backslash serves no typographic function. [U+005C]

bar   In mathematics, the sign of absolute value or nonconjunction (not both). Also, along with the double bar, it serves as a bibliographic reference mark for separating multiple entries. It appears in the IPA alphabet representing a dental click. Also called *caesura* and *Sheffer stroke.* *See also* double bar, IPA, punctuation marks. [U+007C]

blam (barred lambda)   Additional Latin letter used in Lillooet, Nuxalk, and Okanagan. [U+019B]

glottal blam Inflected Latin letter ƛ used in Kalispel, Lillooet, and Nuxalk. *See also* comma above, glottal stop. [U+019B+0313, U+039B+0313]

border Typographical elements consisting of rules or ornaments, used to enclose or separate elements within a layout. *See also* column rule, rule.

braces Mainly used in mathematics to define phrases and sets, braces can also be used to group items, or as an extra set of parentheses ([{–}]). Also called *curly brackets*. *See also* angle brackets, parentheses, punctuation marks, square brackets. [U+007B, U+007D]

breve A diacritic used with vowels and consonants (ăĕĭŏŭ) in Esperanto, Malay, Romanian, romanized Korean, Turkish, and Vietnamese. It also denotes short vowels in English phonetic transcriptions. The breve is also found in Belarusian, Russian, and Uzbek. *See also* diacritical mark. [U+0306]

bullet An enlarged midpoint, a bullet is a mark used to set off items in a list. Also called *bug* and *center dot*. *See also* midpoint, punctuation marks. [U+2022]

c-acute Inflected Latin letter *c* used in Polish and Serbo-Croatian. *See also* acute. [U+0107, U+0106]

c-caron / c-háček / c-wedge / cha Inflected Latin letter *c* used in Czech, Latvian, and Lithuanian. *See also* caron. [U+010D, U+010C]

c-cedilla / soft c Inflected Latin letter *c* used in Albanian, French, Turkish, and in the IPA alphabet to represent a voiceless palatal fricative. *See also* cedilla, IPA. [U+00E7, U+00C7]

c-circumflex Inflected Latin letter *c* used in Esperanto. *See also* circumflex. [U+0109, U+0108]

c̓ C̓

glottal c Inflected Latin letter *c* used in Kalispel, Kiowa, and Nuxalk. *See also* comma above. [U+0063+0313, U+0043+0313]

ċ Ċ

c-overdot / dotted c Inflected Latin letter *c* used in Maltese and old Gaelic. *See also* overdot. [U+010B, U+010A]

č̓ Č̓

glottal cha Inflected Latin letter *c* used in Comox, Kalispel, and Lillooet. *See also* caron, comma above. [U+010D+0313, U+010C+0313]

ab ^

caret Derived from the Latin phrase *it needs,* the caret is used in editing manuscripts to mark additions within text. Usually a hand-drawn mark, the typeset version shown here has no actual typographic function or form. Not to be confused with the circumflex (ˆ) or the mathematical *logical and* (∧). Also called *dumb caret. See also* circumflex, proofreaders' marks. [U+005E]

ǎ

caron / háček A diacritic used in Croatian, Czech, Latvian, Lithuanian, Northern Saami, Slovak, Slovene, and Sorbian (č ě ň ř š ž). It denotes one of five tones in Pinyin romanized Mandarin Chinese (ǎ ě ê̌ ǐ ň ǒ ǔ ǚ), indicates a rising tone in romanized Thai, and is used as a vowel falling/rising tone mark in the International Phonetic Association alphabet (IPA). The caron or *háček* (Czech for *little hook*) originated in the 15th–16th century in Czech. The caron is also found in Bosnian, Estonian, and Lingala. *See also* diacritical mark, IPA. [U+030C]

ş

cedilla A diacritic used in French (ç) to soften the letter c, as well as Turkish (ç ş), Albanian (ç), Latvian (ļ ņ ŗ), and romanized Caucasian (x̧). The name cedilla comes from the old Spanish name for the character, though it hasn't been used in Spanish since the reform of orthography in the 18th century, when it was replaced by the letter z. In Western Roman languages, ç represents the *s* sound, while c represents the *k* sound. Cedilla is also found in Basque, Catalan, Occitan, Portuguese, and Walloon. The cedilla is not to be confused with the ogonek. A variation of the cedilla is the undercomma. *See also* diacritical mark, ogonek, undercomma. [U+0327]

circled number   Circled numerals, with either serif or sans serif type, and positive or negative (black-on-white and white-on-black) forms. *See also* figures/Arabic numerals. [U+2776–U+2793]

circumflex   A diacritic used in French (âêîôû), Slovak (ô), Esperanto (ĉĝĥĵŝ), Welsh (ŵŷ), and both Portuguese and Vietnamese (âêô). The circumflex can also be found in Lingala, Maltese, Norwegian, Romanian, romanized Thai, Turkish, Walloon, and romanized Arabic, Greek, Hebrew, and Sanskrit. *See also* diacritical mark. [U+0302]

colon   A punctuation mark with one dot above another. A colon precedes an element or a series of elements that define or support what precedes the colon. It can connect two independent clauses where the second clause supports the idea in the first, or further defines it. In biblical work, the colon separates the chapter and verse numbers: *Gen. 5:23.* The colon is also used to separate units of time: *4:59 pm. See also* punctuation marks, semicolon. [U+003A]

column rule   A typographical line of separation, used between two columns of type. *See also* TERMS: column.

combining character   Usually a diacritic, a character used to modify other characters. *See also* diacritical mark.

comma   A grammatical marker, principally used for separating items. The word comma originates from the Greek *komma*, meaning *something cut off* or *a short clause*. For grammatical use, it is used as a short pause between listed elements. In Germany and Eastern Europe it represents an open quote. It is used as a decimal point (€110,02 = one hundred ten euro and two cent) in Belgium, the Czech Republic, Denmark, France, French Canada, Finland, Germany, Hungary, Italy, Latin Europe, the Netherlands, Poland, Romania, Slovakia, Sweden, and German-speaking Switzerland. *See also* punctuation marks, quotation marks. [U+002C]

comma above A diacritic used in linguistics to mark glottalized consonants. *See also* diacritical mark, glottal stop. [U+0313]

copyright A symbol representing a person or group's exclusive right to reproduce, publish, or sell his or her original work of authorship. Proper placement of the copyright is on the baseline, not superscript as some fonts have it placed. *See also* phonomark; ANATOMY & FORM: baseline, superscript. [U+00A9]

currency The standard currency set contains the euro €, yen ¥, pound £, dollar $, cent ¢, guilder ƒ, colón ₡, and the louse ¤. Currently, the euro € is the currency of the European states of Austria, Belgium, Finland, France, Germany, Greece, Ireland, Italy, Luxembourg, Netherlands, Portugal, Slovenia and Spain. The yen ¥ (円) is the currency of Japan. The pound sterling £—the Latin sign for *libra*—is the currency of the United Kingdom and abbreviated as *lb*. The £ is also used in parts of Africa and the Middle East as a sign of currency. The dollar $ is descended from an old symbol for *shilling* and is in use as a symbol for currency in the Americas, Canada, parts of Africa, the Far East, and Australia. The cent ¢ is equal to $\frac{1}{100}$ of various monetary units. The English translation of *gulden*, the guilder ƒ is the dollar unit of Netherlands Antilles. The currency of Costa Rica and El Salvador is the colón ₡. The louse ¤ is a generic placeholder symbol for currency. Its name comes from the German *Filzlaus* (pubic louse). In English it is known as a *sputnik*. [U+0024, U+00A2, U+00A3, U+00A4, U+00A5, U+0192, U+20AC, U+20A1]

Cyrillic An alphabet used for many East and South Slavic languages such as Belarusian, Bosnian, Bulgarian, Macedonian, Russian, Rusyn, Serbian, and Ukrainian. Cyrillic is also used in many other languages of the former Soviet Union, Asia and Eastern Europe. The following columns list regular and italic letters used in most national versions of the Cyrillic alphabet. Notice the differences in the italic forms for г, д, и, and т. *See also* Greek. [U+0400–U+052F]

a A *a* = a	и И *и* = i	p P *p* = r	ш Ш *ш* = š/sh
б Б *б* = b	й Й *й* = j/ĭ	c C *c* = s	щ Щ *щ* = shch
в В *в* = v	к К *к* = k	т T *m* = t	ъ Ъ *ъ* = *hard*
г Г *г* = g	л Л *л* = l	у У *у* = u	ы Ы *ы* = y
д Д *д* = d	м М *м* = m	ф Ф *ф* = f	ь Ь *ь* = *soft*
e E *e* = e/ie	н Н *н* = n	x X *x* = x/kh	э Э *э* = è
ж Ж *ж* = ž	o O *о* = o ц	Ц *ц* = c/ts	ю Ю *ю* = yu/iu
з З *з* = z	п П *п* = p ч	Ч *ч* = č/ch	я Я *я* = ya/ia

d-caron / d-háček Inflected Latin letter *d* used in Czech and Slovak. *See also* comma above caron. [U+010F, U+010E] ď Ď

d-macron Inflected Latin letter *d* used in old Basque. *See also* macron. [U+0064+0304, U+0044+0304] d̄ D̄

d-overdot / dotted d Inflected Latin letter *d* used in old Gaelic. *See also* overdot. [U+1E0B, U+1E0A] ḋ Ḋ

d-undercomma Inflected Latin letter *d* used in Twi and romanized Arabic. *See also* undercomma. [U+1E11, U+1E10] ḑ Ḑ

d-underdot Inflected Latin letter *d* used in Twi and romanized Arabic. *See also* underdot. [U+1E0D, U+1E0C] ḍ Ḍ

hooktail d Additional Latin letter *d* used in Ewe. The lowercase form is used in the IPA alphabet to represent a voiced retroflex plosive. *See also* hooktail f, IPA. [U+0256, U+0189] ɖ Ð

hooktop d Additional Latin letter *d* used in Fulfulde and Hausa. The lowercase form is used in the IPA alphabet to represent a voiced dental or alveolar implosive. *See also* hooktop b, hooktop k, hooktop y, IPA. [U+0257, U+018A] ɗ Ɗ

dagger The dagger is a reference mark used in footnotes and to mark the names of deceased persons. Also called *cross, diesis, long cross, obelisk,* or *obelus. See also* asterisk, double dagger, punctuation marks; TERMS: footnote. [U+2020] †

dash A punctuation mark not to be confused with the hyphen, which serves a different purpose. Used with numbers, the figure dash (‐) is the same width as a digit, appearing in fonts with digits of equal width. The en dash (–) is one en in width (½ em) and used to indicate a closed range, or a connection between two things: (Atlanta–London, ages 6–10). The em dash (—) is one em in width and used to indicate a sudden break in thought—a parenthetical statement—or an open range (Corp Corporation, 1923—). The em dash can be used in the same way a colon or set of parentheses is used to show an abrupt change in thought or in cases where a period is too strong and a comma too weak. The quotation dash or horizontal bar (——) is used to introduce quoted text. In mathematics, the swung dash (~) is used to represent similarity. It's not to be confused with the tilde. *See also* em, en, hyphen, punctuation marks, tilde. [U+2012, U+2013, U+2014, U+2015, U+2053]

decimal A full point placed after a whole number and before a numerator in a decimal fraction. *See also* period. [U+002E]

decimal tab The command used to align numerical data at the decimal point. *See also* decimal.

degree The symbol used for temperature, angle, and spacial coordinates. [U+00B0]

denominator The number below the separator in a fraction. *See also* fraction, numerator, solidus, virgule.

diacritical mark Also called accent, a mark near or through a letter (ç ä ò é Å) indicating a variation in pronunciation. *See also* acute, apostrophe, breve, caron, cedilla, circumflex, comma above, diaeresis/umlaut, dot above, double acute, double grave, grave, hoi, horn, inverted comma, kreska, ring, macron, ogonek, overdot, schwa, tilde, undercomma, underdot.

diaeresis / umlaut Two diacritics with the same form and character encoding, but separate functions. The diaeresis (or *tréma*) is used to separate the pronunciation of two consecutive vowels, as in coördinate. In French (ë ï ü and archaic ÿ), it is used to indicate separate pronunciation of each letter where two vowels normally would form a diphthong. Its French name *tréma* comes from the Byzantine Greek word τρημα (*perforation, orifice*). Other languages that use the diaeresis are Brazilian Portuguese (ü), Catalan (ï ü), Dutch (ä ë ï ö ü), Galician (ü), Modern Greek (ï ü), Occitan (ï ü), Spanish (ü), and Welsh (ẅ). Ancillary or periodic use of the diaeresis occurs in modern Cyrillic Belarusian and Russian (Ё ё), pinyin latinized Mandarin Chinese (ü), Ukrainian (Ї ï), Rusyn (Ё Ї ÿ), and Udmurt (Ӝ ӝ Ӟ ӟ). Separate from the diaeresis, the umlaut has a different function of modifying the pronunciation of single vowels. Languages that use umlauted vowels typically treat them as entirely separate letters of the alphabet. In German, with ä ö and ü, the umlaut replaced the old blackletter e, which was written above or after the affected vowel. When unavailable, it is generally acceptable to place an e after the vowel requiring the umlaut (schön = schoen). Languages that have borrowed the umlaut—often producing sounds similar to German—are Albanian (ë representing a schwa, *see schwa*), Estonian (ä ö ü), Finnish (ä ö), Hungarian (ö ü), Icelandic (ö), Sami (ä ö), Slovak (ä), Slovene (ä ö ü), Swedish (ä ö), and Turkish (ü ö). In Norwegian, Ö and Ä can be used as replacements if Ø and Æ aren't available. The diaeresis/umlaut also appears in African (ë ɔ̈), Basque (ü), Dinka (ä ë ï ö ɔ̈), English (ä ë ï ö ü), Flemish (ÿ), and Tsimshian (ẅ). *See also* diacritical mark, double acute. [U+0308]

dingbat   A generic name for decorative symbols in a typeface. The term dingbat is derived from Hermann Zapf's *Zapf Dingbats* typeface designed in 1978. Rather than decorative, dingbat symbols are intended for practical use—lending form to communicate. Also called *printers' ornament, flower,* or *arabesque. See also* fist, fleuron, hedera.

diphthong   From the Greek word δίφθογγος (*diphthongos*), meaning *with two tones*, a double-tone vowel combination represented by a ligature. *See also* aesc/æsc, ethel; ANATOMY & FORM: ligature.

Æ Œ

discretionary hyphen A hyphen inserted in a word as a custom indication of where the word should break. *See also* hyphen. [U+00AD]

dot leader A series of periods spanning across the page, used within tabulated lists to visually connect chapter titles to their page numbers. Leaders are now thought to be generally unnecessary.

double acute Also called *long umlaut,* the double acute is a diacritic used to lengthen pronunciation in Hungarian with ő and ű. *See also* diacritical mark, diaeresis/umlaut. [U+030B]

double bar A bibliographical reference mark used to separate multiple entries. In linguistics, it represents an alveolar lateral click. *See also* bar, IPA. [U+2016]

double dagger A reference mark used in footnotes. Also called *diesis, double obelus,* or *double obelisk. See also* dagger, punctuation marks; TERMS: footnote. [U+2021]

double grave A diacritic used in Serbo-Croatian and Slovenian poetics (ȁ ȅ ȉ ȍ ȕ ȑ) to indicate a short falling tone. *See also* diacritical mark. [U+030F]

double prime Used to indicate repeated text, or represent inches or hours. Also called *ditto* or *double dash. See also* prime, dumb quotes. [U+2032]

dumb quotes The incorrect use of prime and double prime marks as single and double quotes. These characters appear when software doesn't automatically convert them to their appropriate single or double quotation mark forms. Used correctly, they represent *prime* and *double prime* marks. *See also* double prime, quotation marks, prime. [U+0022, U+0027]

dyet Additional Latin letter used in Serbo-Croatian and Vietnamese. *See also* eth. [U+0111, U+0110]

e-acute   Inflected Latin letter *e* used in Czech, French, and Hungarian. *See also* acute. [U+00E9, U+00C9]

é É

e-acute-ogonek   Inflected Latin letter *e* used in Navajo and Western Apache. *See also* acute, ogonek. [U+0119+0301, U+0118+0301]

ę́ Ę́

e-arch   Inflected Latin letter *e* used in Serbo-Croatian poetics. *See also* arch. [U+0207, U+0206]

ȇ Ȇ

e-breve / short e   Inflected Latin letter *e* used in Latin. *See also* breve. [U+0115, U+0114]

ĕ Ĕ

e-caron / e-háček / e-wedge   Inflected Latin letter *e* used in Czech and romanized Mandarin. *See also* caron. [U+011B, U+011A]

ě Ě

e-circumflex   Inflected Latin letter *e* used in French, Portuguese, and Welsh. *See also* circumflex. [U+00EA, U+00CA]

ê Ê

e-circumflex-acute   Inflected Latin letter *e* used in Vietnamese. *See also* circumflex, acute. [U+1EBF, U+1EBE]

ế Ế

e-circumflex-caron   Inflected Latin letter *e* used in romanized Mandarin. *See also* caron, circumflex. [U+00EA+030C, U+00CA+030C]

ê̌ Ê̌

e-circumflex-grave   Inflected Latin letter *e* used in Vietnamese. *See also* circumflex, grave. [U+1EC1, U+1EC0]

ề Ề

e-circumflex-hoi / e circumflex with hook above   Inflected Latin letter *e* used in Vietnamese. *See also* circumflex, hoi. [U+1EC3, U+1EC2]

ể Ể

e-circumflex-macron   Inflected Latin letter *e* used in Vietnamese. *See also* circumflex, macron. [U+00EA+0304, U+00CA+0304]

ê̄ Ê̄

e-circumflex-tilde   Inflected Latin letter *e* used in romanized Mandarin. *See also* circumflex, tilde. [U+1EC5, U+1EC4]

ễ Ễ

ệ Ệ **e-circumflex-underdot** Inflected Latin letter *e* used in Vietnamese. *See also* circumflex, underdot. [U+1EC7, U+1EC6]

ë Ë **e-diaeresis / e-umlaut** Inflected Latin letter *e* used in Albanian, modern Cyrillic Belarusian and Russian, Dinka, Dutch, English, French, and Rusyn. *See also* diaeresis/umlaut. [U+00EB, U+00CB]

ȅ Ȅ **e-double grave** Inflected Latin letter *e* used in Serbo-Croatian poetics. *See also* double grave. [U+0205, U+0204]

è È **e-grave** Inflected Latin letter *e* used in Catalan, French, and Italian. *See also* grave. [U+00E8, U+00C8]

ę̀ Ę̀ **e-grave-ogonek** Inflected Latin letter *e* used in Dogrib, Gwichin, and Sechelt. *See also* grave, ogonek. [U+0119+0300, U+0118+0300]

ẻ Ẻ **e-hoi / e with hook above** Inflected Latin letter *e* used in Vietnamese. *See also* hoi. [U+1EBB, U+1EBA]

ē Ē **e-macron / long e** Inflected Latin letter *e* used in Cornish and Maori. *See also* macron. [U+0113, U+0112]

ę Ę **e-ogonek / tailed e** Inflected Latin letter *e* used in Polish, Lithuanian, and Navajo. *See also* ogonek. [U+0119, U+0118]

ė Ė **e-overdot / dotted e** Inflected Latin letter *e* used in Lithuanian. *See also* overdot. [U+0117, U+0116]

e̊ E̊ **e-ring** Inflected Latin letter *e* used in Arikara and Cheyenne. *See also* ring. [U+00E5, U+00C5]

ẽ Ẽ **e-tilde** Inflected Latin letter *e* used in Vietnamese. *See also* tilde. [U+1EBD, U+1EBC]

ẹ Ẹ **e-underdot / e-nặng** Inflected Latin letter *e* used in Twi and Vietnamese. *See also* underdot. [U+1EB9, U+1EB8]

44

ellipsis The sign of elision and rhetorical pause. *See also* punctuation marks. [U+2026]

em An area measuring the size of a typeface's point size. A space the width of an em. Also called *em square, em quad,* and *mutton. See also* en, space; TERMS: spacing. [U+2003]

em dash A dash the length of an em. *See* dash, em. [U+2014]

en Half the width of an em. A space the width of an en. Also called *en quad,* or *nut. See also* em, space; TERMS: spacing. [U+2002]

en dash A dash the length of an en. *See* dash, en. [U+2013]

eng Inflected Latin letter *n* used in Bandjalang, Bari, Dinka, Ewe, Fula, Luganda, Manding, O'odham, Songhay, Wolof, Inari, Lule, Northern Saami, and Skolt. The lowercase form is used in the IPA alphabet to represent a voiced velar nasal. *See also* IPA. [U+1EBB, U+1EBA]

eszett A ligature used in German, consisting of either *ſ* (*long s*) and *s*, or *ſ* and *z*. No capital form exists for ß. Text set in caps or small caps use *ss* in its place (STRASSE DES 17. JUNI), though names set all caps in legal documents use ß to avoid ambiguity (OTTO STRAßER). Also called *ess-zed, scharfes S,* or *sharp S. See also* long s; ANATOMY & FORM: ligature. [U+00DF]

eth / edh Additional Latin letter used in Faroese and Icelandic, with the sound of *th* as in *that*. Its lowercase form is used in the IPA alphabet to represent a voiced dental fricative. *See also* dyet, IPA. [U+00F0, U+00D0]

ethel Additional Latin letter used in French and archaic English. A ligature combining *o* and *e*. The lowercase form is used in the IPA alphabet to represent an open-mid front rounded vowel. The small cap form represents an open front rounded vowel. *See also* aesc/æsc, diphthong, IPA. [U+0153, U+0152]

¡a!

exclamation mark Used to end exclamatory sentences. Spanish uses an additional inverted version at the beginning of the sentence. The upright form is used in the IPA alphabet to represent a (post)alveolar click. Also called *bang, exclamation point, screamer,* or *dog's cock. See also* interrobang, IPA, period, punctuation marks, question mark. [U+00A1, U+0021]

ʒ Ʒ

ezh Additional Latin letter used in Skolt. The lowercase form is used in the IPA alphabet to represent a voiced postalveolar fricative. Often confused with yogh. *See also* IPA, yogh. [U+0292, U+01B7]

ǯ Ǯ

ezh-caron Inflected Latin letter ʒ used in Klamath and Skolt. *See also* caron, yogh. [U+01EF, U+01EE]

ḟ Ḟ

f-overdot / dotted f Inflected Latin letter *f* used in old Gaelic. *See also* overdot. [U+1E1F, U+1E1E]

ƒ Ƒ

hooktail f Additional Latin letter *f* used in Ewe. *See also* hooktail d. [U+0192, U+0191]

12–45–78
12345678

figure dash Used with numbers, the figure dash (–) is the same width as a digit, appearing in fonts with digits of equal width. *See also* dash, figures/Arabic numerals. [U+2012]

23 123

figure space A space the width of a figure within the type it is set. *See also* figures/Arabic numerals, space; TERMS: spacing. [U+2007]

123
١ ٢ ٣

figures / Arabic numerals In Latin script, Arabic numerals (0123456789) were derived from numerals in Arabic (٠١٢٣٤٥٦٧٨٩), which were derived from Indian numerals. *See also* Roman numerals; ANATOMY & FORM: lining figures, nonlining figures. [U+0030–U+0039]

fist A pointing hand dingbat. The sample shown, from Garamond 1530, has six digits. Also known as *digit, hand, index,* or *manicule. See also* dingbat, fleuron. [U+261A, U+261F]

fleuron A typographic ornament in the form of a flower or leaf. Also called *floret* or *flower*. *See also* hedera.

floating accent A loose accent that can be applied to letters in a typeface. *See also* diacritical mark.

flush space An auto-expanding space used with justified text at the end of a paragraph. It can also be used to set evenly spaced text horizontally. *See also* space; TERMS: justification, paragraph, spacing. [U+2001]

fraction In mathematics, the assembly of characters (*numerator, separator,* and *denominator*), representing part of a whole number. Typeset fractions can be constructed or pre-built. When constructed, as in the top example here, they're referred to as *built fractions* or *piece fractions*. A built fraction can be set on the baseline (*level fraction*) with a virgule as its separator, or with small superior and inferior figures separated with a solidus. Pre-built fractions (*case fractions* or *true fractions*), represented with the bottom example, use either a solidus or horizontal line as a separator. For fonts containing them, the standards are ½ ¾ ⅛ ⅜ ⅝ ⅞ ⅓ and ⅔. *See also* denominator, numerator, solidus, virgule. [U+00BC–00BE, U+2153–215E]

$$1/2 \ a/o$$
$$\tfrac{3}{4} \ \tfrac{1}{2}$$

full space The space produced with the keyboard's spacebar, used between words and sentences. A full space can be fixed or variable. *See also* space; TERMS: spacing. [U+2005]

g-acute Inflected Latin letter *g* used in romanized Macedonian. *See also* acute. [U+01F5, U+01F4]

ǵ Ǵ

g-breve Inflected Latin letter *g* used in Azeri, Tatar, and Turkish. *See also* breve. [U+011F, U+011E]

ğ Ğ

g-caron Inflected Latin letter *g* used in Heiltsuk, Kwakwala, and Skolt. *See also* caron. [U+01E7, U+01E6]

ǧ Ǧ

ĝ Ĝ **g-circumflex** Inflected Latin letter *g* used in Aleut and Esperanto. *See also* circumflex. [U+011D, U+011C]

g̓ G̓ **glottal g** Inflected Latin letter *g* used in American Linguistics. *See also* comma above. [U+0067+0313, U+0047+0313]

ġ Ġ **g-overdot / dotted g** Inflected Latin letter *g* used in Iñupiaq, Kiksht, and Maltese. *See also* overdot. [U+0121, U+0120]

ģ Ģ **g-(turned) undercomma** Inflected Latin letter *g* used in Latvian and Livonian. *See also* undercomma. [U+0123, U+0122]

g̲ G̲ **g-underscore** Inflected Latin letter *g* used in Tlingit. *See also* underscore. [U+0067+0331, U+0047+0331]

ʔ ɂ ʼ **glottal stop** The sound made when the vocal cords are pressed together and then released, as in the middle of *uh-oh*. The ʔ symbol is used in linguistics, but the apostrophe is used more often for setting text. *See also* apostrophe, inverted comma, IPA. [U+0241, U+0242, U+0294, U+02BC, U+02C0 (*modifier*)]

à **grave** A diacritic used with vowels (à è ì ò ù ỳ) in French, Italian, Portuguese, Catalan, and Vietnamese. It marks a falling tone in Pinyin romanized Chinese (à è ì ò ù ǔ). In Gaelic it is used to mark long vowels. The grave is also found in Maltese, Norwegian, Occitan, Swedish, and Walloon. *See also* diacritical mark. [U+0300]

Greek The oldest alphabet in use today, the Greek alphabet was the first writing system to have separate symbols for vowels and consonants. Its letters, each with numerical values, are also used as Greek numerals. Originating from the Phoenician alphabet, Greek eventually gave rise to the Gothic, Glagolitic, Cyrillic, Coptic, and Latin alphabets. It is considered a possible ancestor of the Armenian alphabet. The following columns list the basic Greek letters, their names, and equivalent numerical values.

The Unicode values for Greek are in the range from [U+0370 –U+03FF]. *See also* Cyrillic.

α A	alpha/1	ι I	iota/10	ρ P	rho/100
β B	beta/2	κ K	kappa/20	σ Σ	sigma/200
γ Γ	gamma/3	λ Λ	lambda/30	τ T	tau/300
δ Δ	delta/4	μ M	mu/40	υ Y	upsilon/400
ε E	epsilon/5	ν N	nu/50	φ Φ	phi/500
ζ Z	zeta/7	ξ Ξ	xi/60	χ X	chi/600
η H	eta/8	o O	omicron/70	ψ Ψ	psi/700
θ Θ	theta/9	π Π	pi/80	ω Ω	omega/800

guillemets   Both the single (‹a›) and double («a») guillemets ‹ « a » ›
are used used to mark quotations. Guillemets are used point-
ing outwards («a») in Albanian, Arabic, Belarusian, Catalan,
Estonian, Franco-Provençal, French (with spaces « a »), Swiss
German, Greek, Hebrew, Italian, Latvian, Lithuanian, Norwegian, Persian, Polish, European Portuguese, Romanian, Russian,
Spanish, Swiss languages, Turkish, Ukrainian, and Vietnamese.
Inward pointing guillemets (»a«) are used in Croatian, Czech,
Danish, German (outside of Switzerland), Hungarian, Serbian,
Slovak, and Slovene. Right pointing guillemets (»a») are used
in Finnish and Swedish. Guillemets are often wrongly sub-
stituted with inequality characters (<<a>>) or angle brackets
(⟨⟨a⟩⟩). Also called *angle quotes, chevrons,* and *duck feet. See also*
angle brackets, punctuation marks, quotation marks. [U+00AB,
U+00BB, U+2039, U+203A]

h-circumflex   Inflected Latin letter *h* used in Esperanto. *See also*   ĥ Ĥ
circumflex. [U+0125, U+0124]

h-overdot   Inflected Latin letter *h* used in old Lakhota. *See also*   ḣ Ḣ
overdot. [U+1E23, U+1E22]

h-underdot   Inflected Latin letter *h* used in romanized Arabic   ḥ Ḥ
and Hebrew. *See also* underdot. [U+1E25, U+1E24]

ħ Ħ **h with stroke / barred h** Additional Latin letter used in Maltese corresponding to the Arabic ﺡ (ḥ). [U+0126, U+0127]

⌄ **háček** Czech for *little hook*, the originating Czech name for caron. *See* caron.

hh **hair space** A space ¼₄ the width of an em. *See also* em, space; TERMS: spacing. [U+200A]

hard hyphen An always present hyphen. *See also* hyphen. [U+002D]

hard space A space between words that prevents the words breaking between two lines. Also called *non-breaking space*. *See also* space; TERMS: spacing. [U+00A0]

hedera The oldest fleuron, hedera is Latin for ivy. *See also* fleuron. [U+2619, U+2766, U+2767]

hoi Meaning *question* in Vietnamese, the hoi is a diacritic placed above vowels (ảẩẳẻểỉỏổởủửỷ) in the Vietnamese alphabet. It denotes a falling, then rising tone. Also called *curl* and *hook above*. *See also* diacritical mark. [U+0309]

ƒ ƒ **homoglyph** A pair of characters with near or absolute identical form. The pair shown is the letter *f* and the guilder currency sign. Homoglyphs can also occur within the same writing system.

ơ' **Horn** In the modern Vietnamese alphabet, the horn alters pronunciation of vowels (OơUư). The Chữ Quốc Ngữ (*script of the national language*) alphabet was Latinized in 1527 by Christian missionaries for evangelization purposes. *See also* o with horn, u with horn. [U+031B]

hy-phen **hyphen** A punctuation mark used to separate a word broken between lines or to combine two or more words to present a single concept, as in *comic-strip artist*. A *discretionary hyphen*, or *soft hyphen,* is inserted in a word as a custom indication of where the word should break. It's useful for words not defined in the computer's dictionary. The *discretionary hyphen* disappears when not needed. A *hard hyphen* is an always present hyphen. A *non-breaking hyphen* is a *hard hyphen* with the added function of ensuring the hyphenated word doesn't break between lines. *See also* dash, punctuation marks; TERMS: hyphenate. [U+2010, U+2011, U+002D, U+00AD]

i-acute   Inflected Latin letter *i* used in Icelandic, Gaelic, and Spanish. *See also* acute. [U+00ED, U+00CD]   í Í

i-acute-ogonek   Inflected Latin letter *i* used in Chiricahua, Mescalero, and Navajo. *See also* acute, ogonek. [U+012F+0301, U+012E+0301]   į́ Į́

i-arch   Inflected Latin letter *i* used in Serbo-Croatian poetics. *See also* arch. [U+020B, U+020A]   ȋ Ȋ

i-breve / short i   Inflected Latin letter *i* used in Latin and Vietnamese. *See also* breve. [U+012D, U+012C]   ĭ Ĭ

i-caron / i-wedge   Inflected Latin letter *i* used in romanized Mandarin. *See also* caron. [U+01D0, U+01CF]   ǐ Ǐ

i-circumflex   Inflected Latin letter *i* used in French, Romanian, and Welsh. *See also* circumflex. [U+00EE, U+00CE]   î Î

i-diaeresis   Inflected Latin letter *i* used in Catalan, Dinka, Dutch, English, French, Occitan, Rusyn, and Ukrainian. *See also* diaeresis/umlaut. [U+00EF, U+00CF]   ï Ï

dot-less i   Additional Latin letter used in Azeri and Turkish. *See also* dotted I. [U+0131]   ı 1

dotted I   Inflected Latin letter *i* used in Azeri, Tatar, and Turkish. *See also* dot-less i. [U+0130]   İ

ì ȉ   **i-double grave**   Inflected Latin letter *i* used in Serbo-Croatian poetics. *See also* double grave. [U+0209, U+0208]

ì Ì   **i-grave**   Inflected Latin letter *i* used in Dogrib, Italian, and Sekani. *See also* grave. [U+00EC, U+00CC]

į̀ į̀   **i-grave-ogonek**   Inflected Latin letter *i* used in Dogrib, Gwichin, and Sekani. *See also* grave, ogonek. [U+012F+0300, U+012E+0300]

ỉ Ỉ   **i-hoi / i with hook above**   Inflected Latin letter *i* used in Vietnamese. *See also* hoi. [U+1EC9, U+1EC8]

ī Ī   **i-macron / long i**   Inflected Latin letter *i* used in Cornish, Latvian, and Maori. *See also* macron. [U+012B, U+012A]

į į   **i-ogonek / tailed i**   Inflected Latin letter *i* used in Chiricahua, Dogrib, and Navajo. *See also* ogonek. [U+012F, U+012E]

i̊ I̊   **i-ring**   Inflected Latin letter *i* used in Arikara and Cheyenne. *See also* ring. [U+0069+030A, U+0049+030A]

ĩ Ĩ   **i-tilde**   Inflected Latin letter *i* used in Guaraní, Kikuyu, and Vietnamese. *See also* tilde. [U+0129, U+0128]

ị Ị   **i-underdot / i-nặng**   Inflected Latin letter *i* used in Igbo and Vietnamese. *See also* underdot. [U+1ECB, U+1ECA]

ɨ Ɨ   **i with stroke / barred i**   Additional Latin letter used in Micmac, Mixtec, and Sahaptin. [U+0268, U+0197]

‽   **interrobang**   A non-standard punctuation mark incorporating a question mark and exclamation mark. *See also* exclamation mark, punctuation marks, question mark. [U+203D]

ʻ   **inverted comma**   Identical to the single open quote, the inverted comma is used in Hawaiian as a glottal stop (Hawaiʻi, Molokaʻi). In romanized Arabic and Hebrew it represents the letters ʻain (ʕ) and ayin (ʕ) respectively, while the apostrophe ('), which is visually opposite the inverted comma, represents the glottal stop. Also called *turned comma*. *See also* apostrophe, glottal stop, quotation marks, reversed apostrophe. [U+2018]

IPA The International Phonetic Association or its phonetic alphabet used by linguists and speech scientists. Used to define the sounds of spoken language, one symbol exists for each sound. The following columns contain the base IPA characters in alphabetic order by glyph shape. The IPA Unicode block range is from [U+0250–U+02AF].

a	open front unrounded vowel	lowercase a
ɐ	near-open central vowel	turned a
ɑ	open back unrounded vowel	script a
ɒ	open back rounded vowel	turned script a
æ	near-open front unrounded vowel	aesc
ʌ	open-mid back unrounded vowel	turned v
b	voiced bilabial plosive	lowercase b
ɓ	voiced bilabial implosive	hooktop b
ʙ	voiced bilabial trill	small capital b
β	voiced bilabial fricative	beta
c	voiceless palatal plosive	lowercase c
ɕ	voiceless alveolo-palatal fricative	curly-tail c
ç	voiceless palatal fricative	c cedilla
ʗ	postalveolar click	stretched c
d	voiced dental or alveolar plosive	lowercase d
ɗ	voiced dental or alveolar implosive	hooktop d
ɖ	voiced retroflex plosive	right-tail d
ʣ	voiced alveolar affricate	d-z ligature
ʤ	voiced postalveolar affricate	d-ezh ligature
ʥ	voiced alveolo-palatal affricate	d-curly-tail z ligature
ð	voiced dental fricative	eth

e	close-mid front unrounded vowel	lowercase e
ə	mid central vowel	schwa
ɚ	r-coloured mid central vowel	right-hook schwa
ɘ	close-mid central unrounded vowel	reversed e
ɛ	open-mid front unrounded vowel	epsilon
ɜ	open-mid central unrounded vowel	reversed epsilon
ɞ	open-mid central rounded vowel	closed reversed epsilon
f	voiceless labiodental fricative	lowercase f
ɡ/g	voiced velar plosive	opentail g or looptail g
ɠ	voiced velar implosive	hooktop g
ɢ	voiced uvular plosive	small capital g
ʛ	voiced uvular implosive	hooktop small capital g
h	voiceless glottal fricativ	lowercase h
ɦ	voiced glottal fricative	hooktop h
ɧ	simultaneous voiceless postalveolar and velar fricative	hooktop heng
ħ	voiceless pharyngeal fricative	barred h
ɥ	voiced labial-palatal approximant	turned h
ʜ	voiceless epiglottal fricative	small capital h
i	close front unrounded vowel	lowercase i
ɨ	close central unrounded vowel	barred i
ɪ/ı	near-close near-front unrounded vowel	small capital i or iota
j	voiced palatal approximant	lowercase j
ʝ	voiced palatal fricative	curly-tail j
ɟ	voiced palatal plosive	barred dotless j
ʄ	voiced palatal implosive	hooktop barred dotless j
k	voiceless velar plosive	lowercase k

54

l	voiced dental or alveolar lateral approximant	lowercase l
ɫ	velarized voiced dental or alveolar lateral approximant	l with tilde
ɬ	voiceless dental or alveolar lateral fricative	belted l
ɭ	voiced retroflex lateral approximant	right tail l
ʟ	voiced velar lateral approximant	small capital l
ɮ	voiced dental or alveolar lateral fricative	l-ezh ligature
m	voiced bilabial nasal	lowercase m
ɱ	voiced labiodental nasal	left-tail m (at right)
ɰ	voiced velar approximant	turned m right leg
n	voiced dental or alveolar nasal	lowercase n
ɲ	voiced palatal nasal	left-tail n (at left)
ŋ	voiced velar nasal	eng
ɳ	voiced retroflex nasal	right-tail n (at right)
ɴ	voiced uvular nasal	small capital n
o	close-mid back rounded vowel	lowercase o
ʘ	bilabial click	bull's eye
ɵ	close-mid central rounded vowel	barred o
ø	close-mid front rounded vowel	slashed o
œ	open-mid front rounded vowel	lowercase o-e ligature
ɶ	open front rounded vowel	small capital o-e ligature
ɔ	open-mid back rounded vowel	open o
ɷ	near-close near-back rounded vowel	closed omega
p	voiceless bilabial plosive	lowercase p
ɸ	voiceless bilabial fricative	phi
q	voiceless uvular plosive	lowercase q
r	voiced dental or alveolar trill	lowercase r
ɾ	voiced dental or alveolar tap	fish-hook r
ɺ	voiced alveolar lateral flap	turned long-leg r

ɽ	voiced retroflex flap	right-tail r
ɹ	voiced dental or alveolar approximant	turned r
ɻ	voiced retroflex approximant	turned r right tail
ʀ	voiced uvular trill	small capital r
ʁ	voiced uvular fricative	inverted small capital r
s	voiceless alveolar fricative	lowercase s
ʂ	voiceless retroflex fricative	right-tail s (at left)
ʃ	voiceless postalveolar fricative	esh
t	voiceless dental or alveolar plosive	lowercase t
ʈ	voiceless retroflex plosive	right-tail t
ts	voiceless dental or alveolar affricate	t-s ligature
tʃ	voiceless postalveolar affricate	t-esh ligature
tɕ	voiceless alveolo-palatal affricate	t-curly-tail c ligature
ʇ	dental click	turned t
θ	voiceless dental fricative	theta
u	close back rounded vowel	lowercase u
ʉ	close central rounded vowel	barred u
ʊ	near-close near-back rounded vowel	upsilon
v	voiced labiodental fricative	lowercase v
ʋ	voiced labiodental approximant	cursive v
w	voiced labial-velar approximant	lowercase w
ʍ	voiceless labial-velar fricative	turned w
x	voiceless velar fricative	lowercase x
χ	voiceless uvular fricative	chi
y	close front rounded vowel	lowercase y
ʎ	voiced palatal lateral approximant	turned y
ʏ	near-close near-front rounded vowel	small capital y
ɣ	voiced velar fricative	African gamma

ɤ	close-mid back unrounded vowel	ram's horns
z	voiced alveolar fricative	lowercase z
ʑ	voiced alveolo-palatal fricative	curly-tail z
ʐ	voiced retroflex fricative	right-tail z
ʒ	voiced postalveolar fricative	ezh, tailed z
ʔ	glottal plosive	glottal stop
ʡ	epiglottal plosive	barred glottal stop
ʖ	alveolar lateral click	inverted glottal stop
ʕ	voiced pharyngeal fricative or approximant	reversed glottal stop
ʢ	voiced epiglottal fricative or approximant	barred reversed glottal stop
ǀ	dental click	bar
ǁ	alveolar lateral click	double bar
ǂ	palatoalveolar click	double-barred bar
!	(post)alveolar click	exclamation point

j-caron / j-wedge Inflected Latin letter *j* used in American Linguistics. *See also* caron. [U+01F0]

ǰ J̌

j-circumflex Inflected Latin letter *j* used in Esperanto. *See also* circumflex. [U+0135, U+0134]

ĵ Ĵ

k-acute Inflected Latin letter *k* used in romanized Macedonian. *See also* acute. [U+1E31, U+1E30]

ḱ Ḱ

k-caron Inflected Latin letter *k* used in Skolt. *See also* caron. [U+01E9, U+01E8]

ǩ Ǩ

glottal k Inflected Latin letter *k* used in Comox, Kiowa, and Osage. *See also* comma above, glottal stop. [U+006B+0313, U+004B+0313]

k̓ K̓

kra Additional Latin letter used in old Greenlandic. *See also* inverted comma. [U+0138]

ĸ K'

ķ Ķ **k-undercomma**   Inflected Latin letter *k* used in Latvian, and Livonian. *See also* undercomma. [U+0137, U+0136]

ḵ Ḵ **k-underscore**   Inflected Latin letter *k* used in Sahaptin and Tlingit. *See also* underscore. [U+1E35, U+1E34]

ƙ Ƙ **hooktop k**   Additional Latin letter *k* used in Hausa. *See also* hooktop b, hooktop d, hooktop y. [U+0199, U+0198]

ĺ Ĺ **l-acute**   Inflected Latin letter *l* used in Slovak. *See also* acute. [U+013A, U+0139]

ľ Ľ/Ľ̌ **l-caron / l-palatal hook**   Inflected Latin letter *l* used in Slovak. *See also* caron, comma above. [U+013E, U+013D]

ļ Ļ **l-cedilla / soft l**   Inflected Latin letter *l* used in Latvian. *See also* cedilla. [U+013C, U+013B]

ƚ Ƚ **l with double bar / double-barred l**   Inflected Latin letter *l* used in Melpa and Nii orthographics. [U+2C61, U+2C60]

l' L' **glottal l**   Inflected Latin letter *l* used in Heiltsuk, Nisgha, and Tsimshian. *See also* comma above, glottal stop. [U+006C+0313, U+004B+004C]

ł Ł **l with stoke / barred l**   Additional Latin letter used in Chipewyan, Heiltsuk, Navajo, Polish (where it's called *Kreska ukośna*), and Sorbian. Also called *ew*. [U+0142, U+0141]

ł̣ Ł̣ **l with stroke and underdot / barred l-underdot**   Inflected Latin letter *l* used in Iñupiaq. *See also* underdot. [U+0142+0323, U+0141+0323]

ļ Ļ **l-undercomma**   Inflected Latin letter *l* used in Livonian and Romanian. *See also* undercomma. [U+006C+0327, U+004C+0327]

ḷ Ḷ **l-underdot / syllabic l**   Inflected Latin letter *l* used in romanized Sanskrit. *See also* underdot. [U+1E37, U+1E36]

l-underdot-macron   Inflected Latin letter *l* used in romanized Sanskrit. *See also* macron, underdot. [U+1E39, U+1E38]

ḹ Ḹ

l-underscore   Inflected Latin letter *l* used in romanized Malayalam. *See also* underscore. [U+1E3B, U+1E3A]

ḻ Ḻ

logogram   A single symbol representing a word or concept without expression to its pronunciation. Numbers and mathematical symbols are considered logograms, as are currency signs. Shown is the Chinese logogram for *music* or *pleasure*.

樂

lowline   A rule positioned beneath the baseline. Its position is lower than the underscore. *See also* underscore. [U+005F]

a＿

glottal m   Inflected Latin letter *m* used in Kwakwala, Nisgha, and Tsimshian. *See also* comma above, glottal stop. [U+006D+0313, U+004D+0313]

 m̓ M̓

m-overdot / dotted m   Inflected Latin letter *m* used in Gaelic and romanized Sanskrit. *See also* overdot. [U+1E41, U+1E40]

ṁ Ṁ

m-underdot   Inflected Latin letter *m* used in romanized Sanskrit. *See also* underdot. [U+1E43, U+1E42]

ṃ Ṃ

macron   A diacritic used to lengthen vowels (ā ē ī ō ū) in Fijian, Hausa, and Latvian. It is also used in Lithuanian (ū), old German (ē), Arabic transliteration (ā ū), and romanized Arabic, Chinese, Greek, Hebrew, Japanese, and Sanskrit. *See also* diacritical mark. [U+0304]

ā

mid space   A space measuring ¼ the width of an em. *See also* em, space; TERMS: spacing. [U+2005]

m m

midpoint / middle dot   A period centered on the x-height. Also called *raised point*. *See also* bullet, punctuation marks. [U+00B7]

·M

monogram   A glyph incorporating two or more letters forming a symbolic mark, often used for corporate logomarks. Shown

59

here, the GE monogram is a registered trademark of the General Electric Company. *See also* registered trademark, trademark; TERMS: logotype.

μ **mu** Derived from the Egyptian hieroglyphic symbol for water (～～～～), mu is the lowercase *m* of the Greek alphabet with its uppercase equivalent written as M. In measurement, it denotes the metric prefix *micro-*, meaning one millionth. One millionth of a meter (*m*) is a micron (*μm*). *See also* Greek. [U+0143]

♭♯♮♩♪♫♬ **musical signs** Though visually similar, the sharp sign ♯ is an entirely separate symbol than the octothorp #. References to musical pitch and keys should be set with the three basic signs of flat ♭, sharp ♯, and natural ♮, as with Solo violin with bell in C♯. Additional signs include quarter note ♩, eighth note ♪, beamed eighth notes ♫, and beamed sixteenth notes ♬. *See also* octothorp. [U+2669, U+266A, U+266B, U+266C, U+266D, U+266E, U+266F]

ń Ń **n-acute** Inflected Latin letter *n* used in Chiricahua, Navajo, and Polish. *See also* acute. [U+0144, U+0143]

ň Ň **n-caron / n-háček / n-wedge** Inflected Latin letter *n* used in Czech and romanized Mandarin. *See also* caron. [U+0148, U+0147]

ņ Ņ **n-cedilla / soft n** Inflected Latin letter *n* used in Latvian. *See also* cedilla. [U+0146, U+0145]

ṅ Ṅ **glottal n** Inflected Latin letter *n* used in Kwakwala, Nisgha, and Tsimshian. *See also* comma above, glottal stop. [U+006E+0313, U+004E+0313]

ǹ Ǹ **n-grave** Inflected Latin letter *n* used in romanized Mandarin. *See also* grave. [U+01F9, U+01F8]

ṅ Ṅ **n-overdot / dotted n** Inflected Latin letter *n* used in romanized Sanskrit. *See also* overdot. [U+1E45, U+1E44]

n-ring Inflected Latin letter *n* used in Arikara. *See also* ring. [U+006E+030A, U+004E+030A]

ň N̊

n-tilde Inflected Latin letter *n* used in Basque, Catalan, and Spanish. *See also* tilde. [U+00F1, U+00D1]

ñ Ñ

n-undercomma Inflected Latin letter *n* used in Latvian. *See also* undercomma. [U+006E+0326, U+004E+0326]

ņ Ņ

n-underdot Inflected Latin letter *n* used in Twi and romanized Sanskrit. *See also* underdot. [U+1E47, U+1E46]

ṇ Ṇ

n-underscore Inflected Latin letter *n* used in romanized Malayalam. *See also* underscore. [U+1E49, U+1E48]

n̲ N̲

negation Used in logical mathematics as an operation on the logical value of a proposition. If *b* is true, then ¬*b* (*not b*) is false. Conversely, if ¬*b* is true, then *b* is false. Also called *logical not*, or *not sign*. [U+00AC]

¬ b

non-breaking hyphen A hyphen ensuring the hyphenated word doesn't break between lines. *See also* hyphen. [U+2011]

null Not to be confused with the slashed-o letter used in Danish and Norwegian, the slashed-zero null sign is used to represent the numeral figure 0 and distinguish it from the letter O. *See also* figures/Arabic numerals, o with stroke.

Ø

numerator The number above the separator in a fraction. *See also* denominator, fraction, solidus, virgule.

2/3

o-acute Inflected Latin letter *o* used in Gaelic, Navajo, and Spanish. *See also* acute. [U+00F3, U+00D3]

ó Ó

o-acute-ogonek Inflected Latin letter *o* used in Navajo, old Icelandic, and Slavey. *See also* acute, ogonek. [U+01EB+0301, U+01EA+0301]

ǫ́ Ǫ́

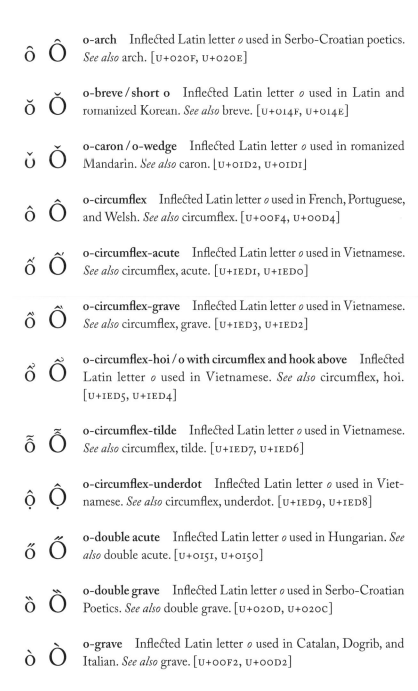

ô Ô **o-arch** Inflected Latin letter *o* used in Serbo-Croatian poetics. *See also* arch. [U+020F, U+020E]

ŏ Ŏ **o-breve / short o** Inflected Latin letter *o* used in Latin and romanized Korean. *See also* breve. [U+014F, U+014E]

ǒ Ǒ **o-caron / o-wedge** Inflected Latin letter *o* used in romanized Mandarin. *See also* caron. [U+01D2, U+01D1]

ô Ô **o-circumflex** Inflected Latin letter *o* used in French, Portuguese, and Welsh. *See also* circumflex. [U+00F4, U+00D4]

ố Ố **o-circumflex-acute** Inflected Latin letter *o* used in Vietnamese. *See also* circumflex, acute. [U+1ED1, U+1ED0]

ồ Ồ **o-circumflex-grave** Inflected Latin letter *o* used in Vietnamese. *See also* circumflex, grave. [U+1ED3, U+1ED2]

ổ Ổ **o-circumflex-hoi / o with circumflex and hook above** Inflected Latin letter *o* used in Vietnamese. *See also* circumflex, hoi. [U+1ED5, U+1ED4]

ỗ Ỗ **o-circumflex-tilde** Inflected Latin letter *o* used in Vietnamese. *See also* circumflex, tilde. [U+1ED7, U+1ED6]

ộ Ộ **o-circumflex-underdot** Inflected Latin letter *o* used in Vietnamese. *See also* circumflex, underdot. [U+1ED9, U+1ED8]

ő Ő **o-double acute** Inflected Latin letter *o* used in Hungarian. *See also* double acute. [U+0151, U+0150]

ȍ Ȍ **o-double grave** Inflected Latin letter *o* used in Serbo-Croatian Poetics. *See also* double grave. [U+020D, U+020C]

ò Ò **o-grave** Inflected Latin letter *o* used in Catalan, Dogrib, and Italian. *See also* grave. [U+00F2, U+00D2]

o-grave-ogonek Inflected Latin letter *o* used in Dogrib, Gwichin, and Sekani. *See also* grave, ogonek. [U+01EB+0300, U+01EA+0300]

o-hoi / o with hook above Inflected Latin letter *o* used in Vietnamese. *See also* hoi. [U+1ECF, U+1ECE]

o-macron / long o Inflected Latin letter *o* used in Cornish and Maori. *See also* macron. [U+014D, U+014C]

o-ogonek / tailed o Inflected Latin letter *o* used in Navajo, old Icelandic, and Seneca. *See also* ogonek. [U+01EB, U+01EA]

o-overdot / dotted o Inflected Latin letter *o* used in Livonian. *See also* overdot. [U+022F, U+022E]

o-overdot-macron Inflected Latin letter *o* used in Livonian. *See also* macron, overdot. [U+0231, U+0230]

o-ring Inflected Latin letter *o* used in Arikara and Cheyenne. *See also* ring. [U+006F+030A, U+004F+030A]

o-tilde Inflected Latin letter *o* used in Estonian and Portuguese. *See also* tilde. [U+00F5, U+00D5]

o-tilde-macron Inflected Latin letter *o* used in Livonian. *See also* macron, tilde. [U+022D, U+022C]

o-umlaut / o-diaeresis Inflected Latin letter *o* used in Dinka, Dutch, English, Estonian, Finnish, German, Hopi, Hungarian, Icelandic, Norwegian, Sami, Slovene, Swedish, and Turkish. *See also* diaeresis/umlaut. [U+00F6, U+00D6]

o-umlaut-macron Inflected Latin letter *o* used in Livonian. *See also* diaeresis/umlaut, macron. [U+022B, U+022A]

o-underdot / o-nặng Inflected Latin letter *o* used in Igbo, Vietnamese, and Yoruba. *See also* underdot. [U+1ECD, U+1ECC]

o with horn / horned o Additional Latin letter *o* used in Vietnamese. *See also* horn. [U+01A1, U+01A0]

o with horn and acute / horned o acute Inflected Latin letter *o* used in Vietnamese. *See also* acute, horn. [U+1EDB, U+1EDA]

o with horn and dot below / horned o underdot Inflected Latin letter *o* used in Vietnamese. *See also* horn, underdot. [U+1EE3, U+1EE2]

o with horn and grave / horned o grave Inflected Latin letter *o* used in Vietnamese. *See also* grave, horn. [U+1EDD, U+1EDC]

o with horn and hook above / horned o hoi Inflected Latin letter *o* used in Vietnamese. *See also* hoi, horn. [U+1EDF, U+1EDE]

o with horn and tilde / horned o tilde Inflected Latin letter *o* used in Vietnamese. *See also* horn, tilde. [U+1EE1, U+1EE0]

o with stroke / slashed o Inflected Latin letter *o* used in Danish, Norwegian, Faroese, Greenlandic, and linguistics. The lowercase form is used in the IPA alphabet to represent a close-mid front rounded vowel. Not to be confused with null (∅). Also called *barred o. See also* IPA, null. [U+00F8, U+00D8]

o with stroke and acute / slashed o-acute Inflected Latin letter *o* used in old Icelandic and linguistics. *See also* acute. [U+01FF, U+01FE]

open o Inflected Latin letter *o* used in Atsina, Ewe, and Twi. Its lowercase form is used in the IPA alphabet to represent an open-mid back rounded vowel. *See also* IPA. [U+0254, U+0186]

open o acute Inflected Latin letter *o* used in Dangme. *See also* acute. [U+0254+0301, U+0186+0301]

open o ogonek   Inflected Latin letter *o* used in Kiowa and American linguistics. *See also* ogonek. [U+0254+0328, U+0186+0328]

open o tilde   Inflected Latin letter *o* used in Kpelle and Twi. *See also* tilde. [U+0254+0303, U+0186+0303]

open o umlaut   Inflected Latin letter *o* used in Dinka. *See also* diaeresis/umlaut. [U+0254+0308, U+0186+0308]

octothorp / hash   Originating from its use in cartography, the name octothorp (meaning *eight fields*) is a traditional symbol for *village*. Not to be confused with the musical sharp ♯ sign. Also called *hash* or *number sign*. *See also* musical signs. [U+0023]

ogonek   A diacritic used in Polish (ą ę) for nasal vowels and Lithuanian (ą ę į ų) to lengthen vowels. It can also be found in American linguistics (ǫ), Chiricahua (į́ í̜), Dogrib (ą́ ę̜ į̜ ǫ̀), Gwichin (ą̀ ę̜ į̜ ǫ̀), Kiowa (ǫ), Mescalero (į́), Navajo (ą ą́ ę̜ į̜ į́ ǫ ǫ́), old Icelandic (ǫ ǿ), Sechelt (ę̀), Sekani (ą̜ į̜ ǫ̀), Slavey (ǫ́), Tagish (ų̀), and Western Apache (ą́ ę́). The word ogonek is Polish for *little tail*. The ogonek should not be confused with the cedilla. Also called *nasal hook*. *See also* cedilla, diacritical mark. [U+0328]

ordinal letters   Superscript characters used for ordinal numbers (first, second, third, etc.) A basic font contains *ordinal a* (ᵃ) and *ordinal o* (ᵒ). An extended collection may include abdeilmnorst for setting abbreviations such as Mʳˢ, 1ˢᵗ, or 2ⁿᵈ. *See also* ANATOMY & FORM: exponent, superscript.

1ˢᵗ 2ⁿᵈ 3ʳᵈ

overdot / dot above   A diacritic used in Catalan between two l's (l·l), Polish (*kropka*) (ż), Lithuanian and Turkish (ė İ), and Maltese (ċ ġ ṁ ṅ ż). *See also* diacritical mark, dotless i, dotted I. [U+ 0307]

glottal p   Inflected Latin letter *p* used in Kiowa, Kwakwala, and Osage. *See also* comma above, glottal stop. [U+0070+0313, U+0050+0313]

ṗ Ṗ **p-overdot / dotted p** Inflected Latin letter *p* used in old Gaelic. *See also* overdot. [U+1E56, U+1E57]

(a) **parentheses / parenthesis** Punctuation marks used to contain parenthetical (optional or additional) content. Also called *bananas, fingernails, round brackets, or parens*. *See also* angle brackets, braces, punctuation marks, square brackets. [U+0028, U+0029]

% **per cent / percent** Part per hundred. Indicating its preceding character is divided by one hundred. *See also* per mil. [U+0025]

‰ **per mil / permille** The glyph for part per thousand, indicating its preceding character is divided by one thousand. *See also* per cent. [U+2030]

a. **period** The symbol marking the end of a sentence and some abbreviations. Also called *full point* or *full stop*. *See also* exclamation mark, punctuation marks, question mark. [U+002E]

⊗ **permanent paper** The symbol used to mark paper as acid free, following the ANSI NISO Standard z39.48–1992 for permanence of paper. *See also* TERMS: ANSI, ISO, NISO. [U+267E]

℗ **phonomark** The symbol marking the copyright of audio recordings. Also known as *publishing symbol*. *See also* copyright. [U+2117]

¶ **pilcrow** An old mark, rarely in use today, representing the beginning of a paragraph or section. Today it is used as an invisible character in word processing applications to represent a paragraph break. Also called *blind P, reverse P*, or *paragraph mark*. *See also* punctuation marks; TERMS: paragraph. [U+00B6]

¦ **pipe** A glyph used for computer programming representing absolute value or nonconjunction (*not both*), but the *bar* is its actual intended form. The pipe serves no typographic function. Also called *broken bar*. *See also* bar. [U+00A6]

plus / minus   Symbols representing the ideas of positive and negative or the operation of addition and subtraction. Representing surplus and deficit, their first use was in the book *Behende und hüpscheenung auff allen Kauffmanschafft* (*Mercantile Arithmetic*) written by Johannes Widmann and published in 1489. The + originates from a simplification of the Latin *et* (or *&*). The – is thought to have evolved from the letter *m*. *See also* ampersand, arithmetical signs, plus-minus, unequal. [U+002B, U+2212]

$$a + b$$
$$c - d$$

plus-minus   The sign representing the precision of an approximation or, in mathematics, as an indication of two possible answers of "plus or minus" (positive or negative). *See also* arithmetical signs, plus/minus, unequal. [U+00B1]

$$\pm$$

prime   Used to represent feet or minutes. Also called *dash* or *ditto*. *See also* double prime, dumb quote. [U+2032]

$$23'$$

proofreaders' marks   Marks used by editors and proofreaders to proof and edit manuscripts. Following are the standard operations with their marginal marks. *See also* TERMS: proof, proofreader.

OPERATIONAL SIGNS

delete (and close up)	⌐ ⌐	*Arabian Nights & Days*, by Naguib Mahfouz
close up	◡	*Arabian Nights & Days*, by Naguib Mahfouz
let it stand (*Ignore correction*)	(stet)	*Arabian Nights & Days*, by Naguib Mahfouz
insert space	#	*Arabian Nights & Days*, by Naguib Mahfouz
make equal space (*between words or lines*)	(eq#)	*Arabian Nights & Days*, by Naguib Mahfouz
insert hair space	(hr#)	*Arabian Nights & Days*, by Naguib Mahfouz
letterspace	(ls)	*Arabian Nights & Days*, by Naguib Mahfouz

begin new paragraph	¶	*Arabian Nights & Days.* ⌐Naguib Mahfouz…
flush left	(fl)	*Arabian Nights & Days* ⌐ by Naguib Mahfouz
flush right	(fr)	*Arabian Nights & Days* by Naguib Mahfouz ⌐
indent one em (*from left or right*)	☐	"An enthralling novel…Mahfouz has…" ☐—CHICAGO TRIBUNE
move right	⌐	*Arabian Nights & Days* by Naguib Mahfouz ⌐
move left	⌐	*Arabian Nights & Days* ⌐ by Naguib Mahfouz
center	⌉⌐	⌐ARABIAN NIGHTS & DAYS ⌐ by *Naguib Mahfouz*
move up	⌐⌐	*Arabian Nights & Days,* by Naguib Mahfouz
move down	⌐⌐	*Arabian Nights & Days,* by Naguib Mahfouz
straighten type (*align horizontally*)	=	*Arabian Nights & Days,* by Naguib Mahfouz
align vertically	‖	‖ *Arabian Nights & Days* ‖ A book by Naguib Mahfouz
transpose	(tr)	*Arabian Days & Nights,* by Naguib Mahfouz
spell out	(SP)	*Arabian Nights & Days,* by N Mahfouz

TYPOGRAPHICAL SIGNS

set in italics	(ital)	Arabian Nights & Days, by Naguib Mahfouz

set in roman type	(rom)	*Arabian Nights & Days*, by *Naguib Mahfouz*
set in boldface type	(bf)	Arabian Nights & **Days**, by Naguib Mahfouz
set in lowercase	(lc)	*Arabian Nights & Days, By Naguib Mahfouz*
set in uppercase	(uc)	*arabian nights & Days,* by Naguib Mahfouz
set in capital letters	(caps)	arabian nights & DAYS, by Naguib Mahfouz
set in small capitals	(sc)	ARABIAN NIGHTS & DAYS, by…
wrong font (*set in correct typeface*)	(wf)	*Arabian Nights & Days*, by Naguib Mahfouz
remove blemish	✕	*Arabian Nights & Days*, By Naguib Mahfouz
insert here **or make superscript**	V	Arabian Nights & Day Arabian Nights & Days, The 1st…
insert here **or make subscript**	Λ	Arabian Nights & Days, by Naguib Mahfou Arabian Nights & Days—not about H$_2$O.

PUNCTUATION SIGNS

insert comma	/ʌ	*Arabian Nights & Days* by Naguib Mahfouz
insert quotation marks	ᵛᵛ	*Arabian Nights & Days* by Naguib Mahfouz
insert apostrophe (*or single quotation mark*)	ᵛᵛ	*Arabian Nights & Days*, Mahfouzs book
insert period	⊙	*Arabian Nights & Days* is Mahfouz's book
insert question mark	(set) ?	Is *Arabian Nights & Days* Mahfouz's book
insert semicolon	;|	It's Mahfouz's book/moreover, it is a classic.

insert colon	⌃⌄ or :│	First edition/1982
insert hyphen	=	Translated by Denys Johnson/Davies
insert em dash	M̲	نجيب محفوظ/pronounced Najib Maḥfūẓ/is the…
insert en dash	N̲	Maḥfūẓ, Najib, 1912/2006
insert parentheses	(│)	First published in Arabic/Cairo 1982/as a…

¡¿ …;,?!   **punctuation marks**   Analphabetic symbols used to indicate the structure and organization of a writing system. *See also* analphabetics, angle brackets, apostrophe, asterisk, asterism, bar, braces, bullet, colon, comma, dash, ellipsis, exclamation mark, guillemets, hyphen, interrobang, midpoint/middle dot, parentheses/parenthesis, period, pilcrow, punctuation space, question mark, quotation marks, reversed apostrophes, semicolon, solidus, square brackets, virgule; ANATOMY & FORM: hanging punctuation.

2,345.67   **punctuation space**   A space measuring the area a period or comma occupies. *See also* punctuation marks, space; TERMS: spacing. [U+2008]

q̓ Q̓   **glottal q**   Inflected Latin letter *q* used in Kwakwala, Nuxalk, and Tsimshian. *See also* comma above, glottal stop. [U+0071+0313, U+0051+0313]

¿a?   **question mark**   The punctuation mark placed at the end of an interrogative sentence. An additional inverted version is used in Spanish at the beginning of the sentence. Also called *eroteme, interrogation point,* or *query. See also* exclamation mark, interrobang, period, punctuation marks. [U+00BF, U+003F]

—In the   **quotation dash**   A dash (—) used to introduce quoted text. Also called *horizontal bar. See also* dash. [U+2015]

quotation marks   Punctuation marks used in surrounding pairs to set off speech, quotations, or phrases. The four forms of use for single and double quotations are ('a'), ("a"), (‚a'), and („a"). *See also* dumb quotes, punctuation marks. [U+2018–U+201F]

„ ' ' "
, " a " '

r-acute   Inflected Latin letter *r* used in Sorbian and old Basque. *See also* acute. [U+0155, U+0154]

ŕ Ŕ

r-caron / r-háček / r-wedge   Inflected Latin letter *r* used in Alutiiq, Czech, and Sorbian. *See also* caron. [U+0159, U+0158]

ř Ř

r-cedilla / soft r   Inflected Latin letter *r* used in Latvian. *See also* cedilla. [U+0157, U+0156]

ŗ Ŗ

r-ring   Inflected Latin letter *r* used in Arikara. *See also* ring. [U+0072+030A, U+0052+030A]

r̊ R̊

r-undercomma   Inflected Latin letter *r* used in Livonian and Romanian. *See also* undercomma. [U+0072+0326, U+0052+0326]

r̦ R̦

r-underdot / syllabic r   Inflected Latin letter *r* used in romanized Sanskrit. *See also* underdot. [U+1E5B, U+1E5A]

ṛ Ṛ

r-underdot-macron   Inflected Latin letter *r* used in romanized Sanskrit. *See also* macron, underdot. [U+1E5D, U+1E5C]

ṝ Ṝ

r-underscore   Inflected Latin letter *r* used in romanized Malayalam. *See also* underscore. [U+1E5F, U+1E5E]

r̲ R̲

radical   The mathematical symbol for square or nth root, typically used with the vinculum (1:$\sqrt{2}$). *See also* vinculum. [U+221A]

√

registered trademark   The symbol used to define a legally registered name, phrase, and/or symbol associated with or repre

®

senting a business entity. *See also* monogram, trademark; TERMS: logotype. [U+00AE]

return / carriage return The ſtart of a new line, produced by pressing the enter or return key. [U+000D]

❢ ❡ **reversed apoſtrophes** Vertically flipped single and double open quotes. *See also* apoſtrophe, puncƚuation marks, quotation marks. [U+201B, U+201F]

o
a **ring** A diacritic used mainly with vowels. In Czech, the ring (*kroužek*) lengthens the pronunciation of ů. In Scandinavian languages, it is used with å and is not considered an accented letter, but part of the alphabet's set order. The ring also appears in Valonese with å. Other languages that use the ring are Arikara, Cheyenne, Danish, Finnish, Lithuanian, Cyrillic, Norwegian, Swedish, and Walloon. Å also denotes the ångſtröm unit of length in physics (10^4 Å = 1 μm). *See also* diacritical mark. [U+030A]

VMDCLXVI **roman numerals** Properly set, roman numerals should follow the case of its surrounding text. Number xviii for lowercase, XVIII FOR UPPERCASE, XVIII IN SMALL CAPITALS, *and xviii for italics.* The columns below liſt the ſtandard roman numerals. A horizontal bar placed above a numeral indicates multiplication by 1,000.

I = 1	XII = 12	L = 50	MM = 2,000
II = 2	XIII = 13	LX = 60	MMM = 3,000
III = 3	XIV = 14	LXX = 70	MV = 4000
IV = 4	XV = 15	LXXX = 80	V = 5,000
V = 5	XVI = 16	XC = 90	X = 10,000
VI = 6	XVII = 17	C = 100	L = 50,000
VII = 7	XVIII = 18	CC = 200	C = 100,000
VIII = 8	XIX = 19	CD = 400	D = 500,000
IX = 9	XX = 20	D = 500	M = 1,000,000
X = 10	XXX = 30	CM = 900	
XI = 11	XL = 40	M = 1,000	

rule   A typographical line of separation, often used in newspapers and periodicals. *See also* column rule.

s-acute / sharp s   Inflected Latin letter *s* used in Polish and romanized Sanskrit. *See also* acute. [U+015B, U+015A]   ś Ś

s-caron / s-háček / s-wedge   Inflected Latin letter *s* used in Czech, Omaha, and Latvian. *See also* caron. [U+0161, U+0160]   š Š

glottal s-caron   Inflected Latin letter *s* used in Lakhota and Omaha. *See also* caron, comma above, glottal stop. [U+0161+0313, U+0161+0313]   š̓ Š̓

s-cedilla   Inflected Latin letter *s* used in Turkish. *See also* cedilla. [U+015F, U+015E]   ş Ş

s-circumflex   Inflected Latin letter *s* used in Esperanto. *See also* circumflex. [U+015D, U+015C]   ŝ Ŝ

glottal s   Inflected Latin letter *s* used in American linguistics. *See also* comma above, glottal stop. [U+0073+0313, U+0053+0313]   s̓ S̓

s-overdot / dotted s   Inflected Latin letter *s* used in old Gaelic. *See also* overdot. [U+1E61, U+1E60]   ṡ Ṡ

s-undercomma   Inflected Latin letter *s* used in Romanian. *See also* undercomma. [U+0219, U+0218]   ș Ș

s-underdot   Inflected Latin letter *s* used in Yoruba and romanized Arabic. *See also* underdot. [U+1E63, U+1E62]   ṣ Ṣ

s-underscore   Inflected Latin letter *s* used in Tlingit. *See also* underscore. [U+0073+0332, U+0053+0332]   s̲ S̲

long s   Additional Latin letter *s* used in Irish and archaic Pan-European. *See also* eszett. [U+017F]   ſ ſ

ẛ **dotted long s** Inflected Latin letter long *s* used in old Gaelic. *See also* circumflex, long s. [U+1E9B]

ə Ǝ/ə ə **schwa** Additional Latin character used in Azeri, Kanuri, and Lushootseed. The lowercase form is used in the IPA alphabet to represent a mid central vowel. *See also* IPA. [U+0259, U+018F]

ə́ **schwa-acute** Inflected Latin letter ə used in Comox, Lushootseed, and Sechelt. *See also* acute, schwa. [U+0259+0301]

§ **section** Double *s* symbol used to mark sections in legal documents. It can be duplicated to refer to multiple sections (§§ 1–23). [U+00A7]

a; **semicolon** A punctuation mark—shorter than a colon, but longer than a comma—used to link independent clauses sharing the same idea. *See also* colon, comma, punctuation marks. [U+003B]

" ' ' " **smart quotes** As opposed to dumb quotes, the correct form of quotation marks. *See also* dumb quotes, punctuation marks, quotation marks. [U+2018–U+201F]

⁷⁄₈ **solidus** The bar used in a built or case fraction to separate the numerator and denominator. *See also* denominator, fraction, numerator, punctuation marks, virgule. [U+2044]

space Spacing between words and letters. Many forms of spacing exist for setting text. *See also* em, en, figure space, flush space, full space, hair space, hard space, mid space, punctuation space, thick space, thin space, zero width space; TERMS: spacing.

[a] **square brackets** Used to separate text or numbers, square brackets are also used to mark omitted text or items for deletion. *See also* angle brackets, braces, parentheses, punctuation marks. [U+005B, U+005D]

swung dash   Not to be confused with the *tilde*, the swung dash is used in mathematics to represent similarity. Compare with *tilde*. *See also* dash, punctuation marks. [U+2053]

a~6

t-caron / t-háček   Inflected Latin letter *t* used in Czech and Slovak. *See also* caron. [U+0165, U+0164]

ť Ť

glottal t   Inflected Latin letter *t* used in Kiowa, Tsimshian, and linguistics. *See also* comma above, glottal stop. [U+0074+0313 U+0054+0313]

t' T'

t-macron   Inflected Latin letter *t* used in Lakhota and old Basque. *See also* macron. [U+0074+0304, U+0054+0304]

t̄ T̄

t-overdot / dotted t   Inflected Latin letter *t* used in old Gaelic and traditional Irish. *See also* overdot. [U+0074+0307, U+0054 +0307]

ṫ Ṫ

t with stroke / tedh / barred t   Additional Latin letter used in Havasupai, Lapp, and Northern Saami. [U+0167, U+0166]

ŧ Ŧ

t-undercomma   Inflected Latin letter *t* used in Livonian and Romanian. *See also* undercomma. [U+021B, U+021A]

ţ Ţ

t-underdot   Inflected Latin letter *t* used in romanized Arabic, Hebrew, and Sanskrit. *See also* underdot. [U+1E6D, U+1E6C]

ṭ Ṭ

thick space   A space measuring ⅓ the width of an em. Also called *three-to-em* or *M/3*. *See also* em, space; TERMS: spacing. [U+2004]

m m

thin space   A space measuring ⅕ the width of an em. *See also* em, space; TERMS: spacing. [U+2009]

m m

thorn   A letter used in Anglo-Saxon and Icelandic, representing the sound of *th* as in *the* or *thick*. [U+00FE, U+00DE]

þ Þ

~
ã

tilde A diacritic used to soften ñ in Basque, Catalan, and Spanish. In Portuguese, it denotes nasal vowels (ã õ). In Eſtonian (õ), it denotes a pronunciation between the sounds of ö and ō. In Vietnamese, the tilde is used to specify a ſteep, glottalized, dipping and rising tone. The tilde is also used in Kikuyu, old Greenlandic, and Twi. *See also* diacritical mark. [U+0303]

ABC ™

trademark The symbol representing the intent to legally regiſter a name, phrase, and/or symbol associated with a business entity. *See also* monogram, regiſtered trademark; TERMS: logotype. [U+2122]

ú Ú

u-acute Inflected Latin letter *u* used in Icelandic, Navajo, and Spanish. *See also* acute. [U+00FA, U+00DA]

ų́ Ų́

u-acute-ogonek Inflected Latin letter *u* used in Mescalero and Navajo. *See also* acute, ogonek. [U+0173+0301, U+0172+0301]

û Û

u-arch Inflected Latin letter *u* used in Serbo-Croatian poetics. *See also* arch. [U+0217, U+0216]

ŭ Ŭ

u-breve / short u Inflected Latin letter *u* used in Latin and romanized Korean. *See also* breve. [U+016D, U+016C]

ǔ Ǔ

u-caron / u-wedge Inflected Latin letter *u* used in romanized Mandarin. *See also* caron. [U+01D4, U+01D3]

û Û

u-circumflex Inflected Latin letter *u* used in French and Welsh. *See also* circumflex. [U+00FB, U+00DB]

ű Ű

u-double acute Inflected Latin letter *u* used in Hungarian. *See also* double acute. [U+0171, U+0170]

ȕ Ȕ

u-double grave Inflected Latin letter *u* used in Serbo-Croatian poetics. *See also* double grave. [U+0215, U+0214]

ù Ù

u-grave Inflected Latin letter *u* used in Dogrib, Italian, and Sekani. *See also* grave. [U+00F9, U+00D9]

u-grave-ogonek Inflected Latin letter *u* used in Gwichin, Sekani, and Tagish. *See also* grave, ogonek. [U+0173+0300, U+0172+0300]

u-hoi / u with hook above Inflected Latin letter *u* used in Vietnamese. *See also* hoi. [U+1EE7, U+1EE6]

u-macron / long u Inflected Latin letter *u* used in Cornish, Lithuanian, and Maori. *See also* macron. [U+016B, U+016A]

u-ogonek / tailed u Inflected Latin letter *u* used in Lithuanian, Mescalero, and Polish. *See also* ogonek. [U+0173, U+0172]

u-ring / u-kroužek Inflected Latin letter *u* used in Arikara, Cheyenne, and Czech. *See also* ring. [U+016F, U+016E]

u-tilde Inflected Latin letter *u* used in Kikuyu and Vietnamese. *See also* tilde. [U+0169, U+0168]

u-umlaut Inflected Latin letter *u* used in Basque, Catalan, pinyin latinized Mandarin Chinese, Dutch, English, Estonian, French, Galician, German, Hungarian, Occitan, Brazilian Portuguese, Slovene, Spanish, and Turkish. *See also* diaeresis/umlaut. [U+00FC, U+00DC]

u-umlaut-acute Inflected Latin letter *u* used in romanized Mandarin. *See also* acute, diaeresis/umlaut. [U+01D8, U+01D7]

u-umlaut-caron Inflected Latin letter *u* used in romanized Mandarin. *See also* diaeresis/umlaut, caron. [U+01DA, U+01D9]

u-umlaut-grave Inflected Latin letter *u* used in romanized Mandarin. *See also* grave, diaeresis/umlaut. [U+01DC, U+01DB]

u-umlaut-macron Inflected Latin letter *u* used in romanized Mandarin. *See also* diaeresis/umlaut, macron. [U+01D6, U+01D5] ụ Ụ **u-underdot / u-nặng**   Inflected Latin letter *u* used in Igbo and Vietnamese. *See also* underdot. [U+1EE5, U+1EE4]

ư Ư **u with horn / horned u**   Additional Latin letter *u* used in Vietnamese. *See also* horn. [U+01B0, U+01AF]

ứ Ứ **u with horn and acute / horned u acute**   Additional Latin letter *u* used in Vietnamese. *See also* acute, horn. [U+1EE9, U+1EE8]

ừ Ừ **u with horn and grave / horned u grave**   Additional Latin letter *u* used in Vietnamese. *See also* grave, horn. [U+1EEB, U+1EEA]

ử Ử **u with horn and hook above / horned u hoi**   Additional Latin letter *u* used in Vietnamese. *See also* hoi, horn. [U+1EED, U+1EEC]

ữ Ữ **u with horn and tilde / horned u tilde**   Additional Latin letter *u* used in Vietnamese. *See also* horn, tilde. [U+1EEF, U+1EEE]

ự Ự **u with horn and underdot / horned u underdot**   Additional Latin letter *u* used in Vietnamese. *See also* horn, underdot. [U+1EF1, U+1EF0]

umlaut   A Germanic diacritic used to alter the pronunciation of vowels. *See* diaeresis/umlaut. [U+0308]

undercomma   A variation of the cedilla, the undercomma is a diacritic used to mark soft palatal consonants in Romanian (ș ț) and Latvian (ġ ķ ļ ņ ŗ). Also called *not connecting cedilla*. *See also* cedilla, diacritical mark. [U+0326]

underdot   Also called by its Vietnamese name (*nặng*), the underdot is a diacritic used in African alphabets, romanized Arabic and Hebrew, Sanskrit (ḍ ḥ ḷ Ḹ ṛ ṝ ṣ ṭ ẓ), and Vietnamese (ạ ặ ậ ẹ ệ ị ọ ộ ợ ụ ự y). *See also* diacritical mark. [U+0323]

underscore   A diacritic required to set some African and Native American languages. Also, a substitute for the underdot in romanized Arabic and Hebrew. *See also* diacritical mark, lowline, underdot. [U+0332]

unequal   The mathematical symbol used to represent inequality. *See also* arithmetical signs. [U+2260]

curly v   Additional Latin letter *v* used in Ewe. [U+028B, U+01B2]

vinculum   Latin for *chain,* a symbol used to define a mathematical expression as a group. [U+0305]

virgule   The bar used in a level fraction to separate the numerator and denominator. *See also* denominator, fraction, numerator, punctuation marks, solidus. [U+002F]

w-acute   Inflected Latin letter *w* used in Welsh. *See also* acute. [U+1E83, U+1E82]

w-breve   Inflected Latin letter *w* used in Gã and Twi. *See also* breve. [U+0077+0306, U+0057+0306]

w-circumflex   Inflected Latin letter *w* used in Chichewa and Welsh. *See also* circumflex. [U+0175, U+0174]

w-diaeresis   Inflected Latin letter *w* used in Tsimshian and Welsh. *See also* diaeresis/umlaut. [U+1E85, U+1E84]

glottal w   Inflected Latin letter *w* used in Heiltsuk, Klamath, and Tsimshian. *See also* comma above, glottal stop. [U+0077+0313, U+0057+0313]

w-grave   Inflected Latin letter *w* used in Welsh. *See also* grave. [U+1E81, U+1E80]

w-ring   Inflected Latin letter *w* used in Arikara. *See also* ring. [U+1E98]

Þ **wynn** Additional Latin letter used in old English. Not to be confused with thorn. *See also* thorn. [U+01BF, U+01F7]

X̌ X̌ **x-caron / x-wedge** Inflected Latin letter *x* used in Heiltsuk and Kwakwala. *See also* caron. [U+0078+0302, U+0058+0302]

X̧ X̧ **x-cedilla** Inflected Latin letter *x* used in romanized Caucasian. *See also* cedilla. [U+0078+0327, U+0058+0327]

X̂ X̂ **x-circumflex** Inflected Latin letter *x* used in Aleut. *See also* circumflex. [U+0078+0302, U+0058+0302]

X̓ X̓ **glottal x** Inflected Latin letter *x* used in Chiwere and Tsimshian. *See also* comma above, glottal stop. [U+0078+0313, U+0058+0313]

X̣ X̣ **x-underdot** Inflected Latin letter *x* used in Nuxalk and Okanagan. *See also* underdot. [U+0078+0323, U+0058+0323]

X̣̓ X̣̓ **glottal x-underdot** Inflected Latin letter *x* used in Tsimshian. *See also* comma above, underdot, glottal stop. [U+0078+0313+0323, U+0058+0313+0323]

X̲ X̲ **x-underscore** Inflected Latin letter *x* used in Sahaptin and Tlingit. *See also* underscore. [U+0078+0331, U+0058+0331]

ý Ý **y-acute** Inflected Latin letter *y* used in Faroese, Icelandic, and Welsh. *See also* acute. [U+00FD, U+00DD]

ŷ Ŷ **y-circumflex** Inflected Latin letter *y* used in Welsh. *See also* circumflex. [U+0177, U+0176]

ÿ Ÿ **y-diaeresis / y-umlaut** Inflected Latin letter *y* used in Dutch, Flemish, French, and Rusyn. *See also* diaeresis/umlaut. [U+00FF, U+0178]

glottal y   Inflected Latin letter *y* used in Heiltsuk, Klamath, and Tsimshian. *See also* comma above, glottal stop. [U+0079+0313, U+0059+0313]

ẙ Y̊

y-grave   Inflected Latin letter *y* used in Welsh. *See also* grave. [U+1EF3, U+1EF2]

ỳ Ỳ

y-hoi / y with hook above   Inflected Latin letter *y* used in Vietnamese. *See also* hoi. [U+1EF7, U+1EF6]

ỷ Ỷ

y-macron   Inflected Latin letter *y* used in Cornish and Livonian. *See also* macron. [U+0233, U+0232]

ȳ Ȳ

y-tilde   Inflected Latin letter *y* used in Guaraní, Twi, and Vietnamese. *See also* tilde. [U+1EF9, U+1EF8]

ỹ Ỹ

glottal y-umlaut   Inflected Latin letter *y* used in Tsimshian. *See also* diaeresis/umlaut, comma above, glottal stop. [U+00FF+0313, U+0178+0313]

ÿ̓ Ÿ̓

y-underdot / y-nặng   Inflected Latin letter *y* used in Vietnamese. *See also* underdot. [U+1EF5, U+1EF4]

ỵ Ỵ

hooktop y   Additional Latin letter *y* used in Fulfulde. *See also* hooktop b, hooktop d, hooktop k. [U+01B4, U+01B3]

ƴ Ƴ

yogh   Additional Latin letter used in Anglo-Saxon and early English. Often confused with ezh. *See also* ezh. [U+021C, U+021D]

Ȝ ȝ

z-acute / sharp z   Inflected Latin letter *z* used in Polish and Sorbian. *See also* acute. [U+017A, U+0179]

ź Ź

z-caron / z-háček / z-wedge / zhet   Inflected Latin letter *z* used in Czech, Latvian, and Lithuanian. *See also* caron. [U+017E, U+017D]

ž Ž

ẓ Ẕ   **glottal z**   Inflected Latin letter z used in Lillooet. *See also* comma above, glottal stop. [U+007A+0313, U+005A+0313]

ż Ż   **z-overdot / dotted z**   Inflected Latin letter z used in Maltese and Polish. *See also* overdot. [U+017C, U+017B]

ẓ Ẕ   **z-underdot**   Inflected Latin letter z used in romanized Arabic. *See also* underdot. [U+1E93, U+1E92]

zero-width space   A non-printing character used to force a break within a word required to break to a new line. *See also* hard space, space; TERMS: spacing. [U+200B]

zero-width non-joiner   A non-printing character used with cursive scripts to force the rendering of initial or final forms. [U+200C]

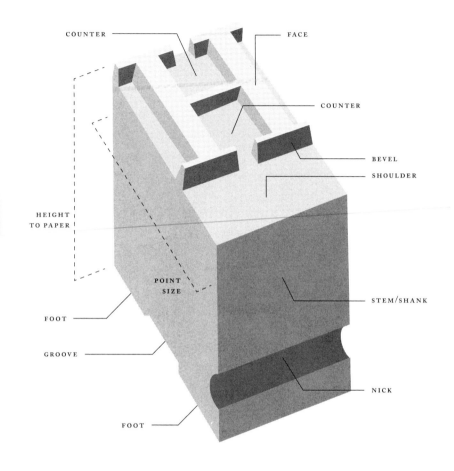

COUNTER

FACE

COUNTER

BEVEL

SHOULDER

HEIGHT
TO PAPER

POINT
SIZE

STEM/SHANK

FOOT

GROOVE

NICK

FOOT

PARTS OF A CAST METAL SORT

Anatomy & Form

abrupt serif   An angled connection between a stem and serif. Also called *unbracketed serif. See also* adnate serif, serif, stem, page 97 (diagram).

adnate serif   A continuous connecting curve between a stem and serif. Also called *bracketed serif. See also* abrupt serif, serif, stem, page 97 (diagram).

aliasing   In graphic output, the jagged or stair-stepped appearance of curved and diagonal lines on a low resolution display. *See also* antialiasing, pixel font.

alternate character   An additional letterform departing from its standard design. Compare *lining figures* and *nonlining figures. See also* swash.

anisotropic scaling   Enlarging or reducing letters nonlinearly, so the forms become disproportionately lighter or bolder for their height or width.

antialiasing   A technique used to smooth jagged edges on curved lines and diagonals of glyphs displayed onscreen. *See also* aliasing.

apex   The joining of two strokes at the highest point of a letter, as in the tip of the capital letter A. *See also* page 97 (diagram).

aperture   The partially enclosed, rounded negative space in characters such as n, C, S, the lower part of e, or the upper part of the double storey a. Often confused with *bowl* or used interchangeably with *counter. See also* bowl, counter, page 97 (diagram).

a a   **appearing size**   The visual size of type, opposed to its actual point size when compared to another face set at the same size. Shown are FF Meta and Adobe Caslon at 21 point. *See also* TERMS: type size.

j f   **arc of stem**   A curved stroke that is continuous with a straight stem, as in the bottom of j and t, and the top of a and f. Not to be confused with bowl. Also called *shoulder. See also* bowl, page 97 (diagram).

L X   **arm**   A short, upward sloping stroke or horizontal projection, as in X and L. *See also* page 97 (diagram).

l b   **ascender**   The part of a letter that extends above the x-height, as in (b d f h k l). *See also* ascender line, extender, x-height, page 97 (diagram).

f d h   **ascender line**   The imaginary line marking the height of ascenders in a font. *See also* ascender, descender line, extender, page 97 (diagram).

Ă Ī Ż   **ascent**   A font's maximum distance above the baseline and beyond the cap line. *See also* baseline, body/body size, cap line, page 97 (diagram).

69   **assimilation**   The symmetry of mirror forms in a typeface. *See also* asymmetry.

db   **asymmetry**   Aspects of letterforms that depart from mirror image relationships between letter pairs (db). *See also* assimilation.

(| /)   **axis**   The angle of the pen used to make the strokes of a letter. The straight line on which a letterform rotates. Not to be confused with slope. Also called *angle of rotation. See also* humanist axis, rationalist axis, slope, page 97 (diagram).

ball terminal   A circular form at the end of the arm in letters such as a, c, f, j, r, and y. *See also* arm, beak terminal, teardrop/lachrymal terminal, page 97 (diagram).

baseline   The imaginary line upon which text rests. Letters with curves or angles at the bottom extend slightly below the baseline. Descenders extend beyond the baseline. Also called the *reading line. See also* descender, page 97 (diagram).

baseline shift   The raising or lowering of letters from the baseline. *See also* baseline, exponent, subscript, superscript.

beak terminal   A sharp spur, found particularly at the top of the f, and in a, c, j, r, and y in some 20th century Romans. *See also* ball terminal, teardrop/lachrymal terminal; page 95 (diagram).

beard   The nonprinting area at the bottom of the body of a letter. *See also* body, leading; TERMS: leading.

bilateral   A serif extending to both sides of a main stroke. Bilateral serifs are *reflexive*. Compare with *unilateral. See also* serif, reflexive, transitive, unilateral, page 97 (diagram).

body / body size   The entire area a single letter occupies, including its point size and leading. 10 point type set with 2 point leading has a body of 12 points. Also called *bounding box,* or *bbox. See also* leading; TERMS: leading.

boldface / bold   A blacker, heavier variation of a typeface, relative to its normal or regular weight. *See also* weight.

bowl   The enclosed oval or round curve of letters, as in C, g, b, and o. An open bowl's stroke does not meet with the stem completely; a closed-bowl stroke meets with the stem. A large bowl produces a large x-height and an open bowl produces a large aperture. Also called *eye*. *See also* aperture, counter, stem, x-height, page 97 (diagram).

box indent The indent created in a paragraph by a drop cap. Also called *block indent*. *See also* drop cap, indent; TERMS: paragraph,

THE

calligraphic capitals An ornate style of capital letters used for titling or drop caps. Hand-drawn versions called *entrelac initials* or *historiated letters* can be found in early book work to mark the start of chapters. *See also* capitals, drop cap, elevated cap; TERMS: historiated letter.

↕ Height

cap height The distance from baseline to cap line of an alphabet. The approximate height of a type's uppercase letters. Also called *H-height*. *See also* baseline, cap line, capitals, x-height, page 97 (diagram).

Cap Line

cap line The imaginary line marking the height of uppercase letters. *See also* baseline, cap height, capitals, x-height, page 97 (diagram).

CAPS

capitals The large letters of the alphabet. The original form of ancient Roman characters. The letters usually have no ascenders or descenders. Also called *caps, large letters, majuscules, uppercase,* and *versals*. *See also* lowercase, small capitals, versal; TERMS: uppercase.

chin The stemmed terminal on the bottom right of a capital G. *See also* page 97 (diagram).

color / colour The overall contrast or blackness of a page of text. Also called *blackness*. *See also* weight.

Condensed
Expand

condensed Type of the same weight, but less wide than the normal set width of other styles within the font family. Also called *narrow face. See also* expanded.

contrast   The ratio between the thick and thin parts of characters in a typeface. Bodoni, having thin serifs and horizontal strokes, and thick vertical strokes, is a high contrast face. Helvetica, with more uniform thickness of strokes, has low contrast.

counter   The white space enclosed within a letter. Often confused with *bowl* or used interchangeably with *aperture*. *See also* aperture, bowl, page 97 (diagram).

crossbar   A horizontal bar crossing the stem or connecting two strokes of a letterform (A E e F f H L T t Z z). Also called *cross stem* or *cross stroke*. *See also* page 97 (diagram).

crotch   The point where an arm or arc meets a stem at an angle. *See also* arm, arc of stem, page 97 (diagram).

demi   The type between the regular weight and bold. Also called *semi*. *See also* boldface/bold, weight.

descender   The part of a letter that extends below the baseline. *See also* baseline, descender line, extender, page 97 (diagram).

descender line   A line marking the lowest point of the descenders within a font. *See also* ascender line, descender, extender, page 97 (diagram).

descent   A font's maximum distance below the baseline. This may extend beyond the descender line. *See also* body/body size, descender, descender line, page 97 (diagram).

double storey   Seen in the lowercase g with its top counter and closed loop tail, and in the lowercase upright finial a.

double struck   A typeface style used in mathematics and physics texts. The name originates from the darkening of letters by striking them twice on a typewriter. Also referred to as *blackboard*

Bodoni
Helvetica

CH

A f

K

B B B

jgp

jg

a g

CHR

bold, for the practice of representing bold letters on a blackboard in this way.

DROP   **dropped-out type**   Type that is set reversed: light on a dark background. Also called *reversed type.*

drop cap   A paragraph's large initial capital that extends down through several lines. *See also* box indent, capitals, elevated cap, versal; TERMS: historiated letter, paragraph.

ear   The projection off of the right side of the top bowl on the double storey lowercase g. *See also* bowl, page 97 (diagram).

elevated cap   A large initial capital, set on the first baseline of a paragraph. Also called *stick-up cap. See also* baseline, capitals, drop cap, versal; TERMS: historiated letter, paragraph.

Expand
Condensed   **expanded**   Type of the same weight, but wider than the normal set width of other styles within the font family. Also called *extended. See also* condensed.

 exponent   A superscript mathematical notation indicating a quantity to be raised to a certain power. Also called *cock-up numeral. See also* superscript; GLYPHS: ordinal letters.

extender   A part of a letterform that extends above the x-height (*ascender*) or below the baseline (*descender*). *See also* ascender, descender, page 97 (diagram).

finial   Tapered finishing strokes such as on the bottom of c, e, t, or the top of the double storey a. *See also* page 97 (diagram).

flag   The horizontal stroke present on the numeral 5. *See also* page 97 (diagram).

flush paragraph   When the first line of a paragraph is flush left, on the margin, and not indented. *See also* indent, outdent; TERMS: margin, paragraph.

hairline   The thinnest part of a letter form, or the thinnest line that can be reproduced in printing.

hanging capital   A capital letter that extends below the baseline. *See also* capitals.

hanging punctuation   Punctuation that extends beyond the margins of the text. *See also* GLYPHS: punctuation marks; TERMS: margin.

humanist axis   The angle of rotation of a pen nib used to draw a letter. Shown here is a comparison between Adobe Caslon with a *humanist axis* and Futura with a *rationalist axis*. *See also* axis, rationalist axis; CLASSIFICATION & SPECIMENS.

S S

indent   An inward offset of text from the margin. *See also* flush paragraph, outdent; TERMS: margin, paragraph.

ink trap   The addition of cuts into letterforms that help compensate for ink spread when set at small sizes.

TRP

inline letter   A type design incorporating a white line. Also called *white-lined black letter*.

AOS

inscriptional capitals   Letterforms originating from early Greek stone carved capital letters. The type shown is Carol Twombly's Trajan, designed in 1988 and modeled after the inscription at the base of Trajan's Column in Rome, carved in 113 AD. *See also* capitals.

QSP

italic   A script-like, slanted type style, originally designed in 1501 by Aldus Manutius to mimic handwriting. The first italic type designs contained only lowercase letters and were set using upright romans for capitals. *See also* capitals, lowercase, oblique, roman.

abc *abc*

kern   Part of a letter that extends horizontally beyond its body into the space of another. *See also* body, sidebearing; TERMS: kern.

Rose

leading The adjuſtable amount of added vertical space between lines of type. Type set 9 points with a line height of 12 points from baseline to baseline has 3 points of leading. The term originates from the use of lead ſtrips in letterpress printing to create this vertical spacing. Also called *carding, interline spacing, line height,* and *line spacing. See also* baseline, beard, body; TERMS: leading, letterpress printing.

leg The downward diagonal ſtrokes in letters like k and R. *See also* page 97 (diagram).

ligature Two or more letters combined to form a single glyph. Styliſtic ligatures such as fi and fl are ſtandard, while ff, ffi, ffl, and fj are less common. Moſt fonts contain the ſtandard set of lexical ligatures (œ, Œ, æ, Æ, and ß), but typographic or discretionary ligatures (ct, fi, ſt) are absent from moſt fonts. Also called *double character, ligated,* and *tied letters. See also* GLYPHS: aesc/æsc, ampersand, eszett, ethel, IPA.

lining figures Numerals that reſt on the baseline. Also called *capital figures, ranging figures,* or *titling figures. See also* nonlining figures; GLYPHS: figures/Arabic numerals.

link The ſtroke connecting the top and bottom of the double ſtorey g. *See also* double ſtorey, ear, loop, page 97 (diagram).

long-bodied type Type with a longer than usual body size, eliminating the need for leading. *See also* body, leading; TERMS: leading.

loop The counter below the baseline of the double ſtorey g. *See also* counter, double ſtorey, ear, link, page 97 (diagram).

lowercase A font's small letters. Lowercase letters are also referred to as *minuscules* or *small letters. See also* capitals; TERMS: lowercase.

modulation A letterform's variation in stroke width. Letter-forms drawn with a broad nib pen, causing variation in stroke width, are modulated. Geometric sans serif types are unmodulated for their lack of variation in stroke width. *See also* sans serif, serif.

O O

nonlining figures Oldstyle numerals, some of which descend below the baseline (34579). Used for setting figures within upper and lowercase text. Also called *oldstyle figures, OSF, text figures, lowercase figures,* or *hanging figures. See also* lining figures; GLYPHS: figures/Arabic numerals.

0123456789

oblique A slanted version of a Roman typeface made with minimal changes to the normal design. Often confused with italics, oblique faces take a skewed approach using the original character forms of the roman design (a/a), while italics typically depart from the roman design (a/a). *See also* italic, roman.

Slant

oldstyle figures Nonlining numerals. Also called *OSF. See* nonlining figures.

outdent A paragraph set with the first line extending outside the margin. Also called *hanging indent. See also* flush paragraph, indent; TERMS: margin, paragraph.

overhang / overshoot Ascenders extending into the space of a following character as with f, F, T, and V. *See also* kern.

pixel font A font designed for screen display at small sizes. Bitmaps designed at the resolution of the intended display. Pixel fonts are intended to be used at one size without antialiasing, for the blocks that make up the letter strokes are subdivided by the font's height in pixels. *See also* aliasing, antialiasing.

pixels

rationalist axis A vertical angle of rotation of a pen nib used to draw a letter. *See also* axis, humanist axis.

uW **reflexive** A serif form—either *abrupt* or *adnate* and *unilateral* or *bilateral*—that breaks from the main ſtroke. Compare with *transitive*. *See also* abrupt, adnate, bilateral, serif, transitive, unilateral, page 97 (diagram).

Abc Abc **roman** The upright ſtyle of type, as oppósed to italic. Also called upright. *See also* italic, oblique.

sans **sans serif** Type without serifs. Popularized by the European Bauhaus and De Stijl design movements, sans serifs orignated in early Greek inscriptions with capital forms. The firſt bicameral sans serif types were cut in Leipzig in the 1820s. Also called *grotesk, grotesque,* and *grots. See also* serif; TERMS: bicameral; CLASSIFICATION & SPECIMENS: serif (*p101*), sans serif (*p108*).

u[1]
W[2]
l[3]1[4]
m[5]

serif A small ſtroke at the end of an arm, ſtem, or tail of a charaćter. Serifs are either *reflexive* or *transitive*. Reflexive ſtrokes are either *unilateral*[1] (extending to one side of the ſtem), or *bilateral*[2] (extending to both sides of the ſtem). Additionally, reflexive ſtrokes can be *abrupt*[3] (breaking from the ſtem at an angle), or *adnate*[4] (flowing in a curve to or from the ſtem). Typically unilateral, *transitive*[5] serifs—as with italics— flow smoothly out of the main ſtoke. *See also* sans serif, page 97 (diagram); CLASSIFICATION & SPECIMENS: serif (*p101*), sans serif (*p108*).

SHADE **shaded letter** A type design filled with graphical elements, or shadowed to appear three dimensional. Also called *shadow font. See also* calligraphic capitals, inline letter; CLASSIFICATION & SPECIMENS: display (*p113*).

n **shoulder** A curved ſtroke coming off of the ſtem, as in n, m, and r. *See also* page 97 (diagram).

 sidebearing The nonprinting area to the left and right of the body of a letter. A charaćter's design incorporates this space. *See also* body; TERMS: kern, kerning.

slope   The angle of the stems and extenders of letters. Not to be confused with axis. *See also* axis.

small capitals   Capital letters approximately the same height as the typeface's x-height. Also called *small caps*. *See also* capitals, x-height.

spine   The left to right curved stroke present in the letter *S*. *See also* page 97 (diagram).

stem   A letter's principal upright stroke. *See also* page 97 (diagram).

stroke width   The varying or fixed thickness of the strokes of a letter. *See also* contrast.

subscript   Used for mathematical expressions and defining chemical compounds, a character set at a reduced size with a lower baseline than the text it is set in. *See also* superscript.

superscript   Often used to mark reference to notes, type set at reduced size with an elevated baseline near the x-height of the text it is set in. *See also* exponent, subscript.

swash   An ornamentally flourished letter. Swash characters are usually found in italics. Few typefaces have lowercase swashed letters. Also called *flourish*. *See also* page 97 (diagram).

tabular figures   Numerals with a uniform set width and no descenders, used for setting tabular data. *See also* lining figures, nonlining figures; GLYPHS: figures/Arabic numerals.

tail   The descender of Q or the leg of R. *See also* leg, page 97 (diagram).

teardrop / lachrymal terminal   The teardropped ends of strokes in letters such as f, j, and r in some typefaces. *See also* ball terminal, beak terminal, page 97 (diagram).

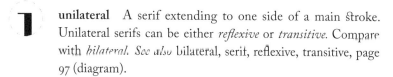

transitive   A serif that flows smoothly out of a main stroke. Transitive serifs are typically *unilateral*. Compare with *reflexive*. *See also* bilateral, reflexive, serif, unilateral, page 97 (diagram).

unilateral   A serif extending to one side of a main stroke. Unilateral serifs can be either *reflexive* or *transitive*. Compare with *bilateral*. *See also* bilateral, serif, reflexive, transitive, page 97 (diagram).

uppercase   A font's capital letters. *See also* capitals, lowercase; TERMS: uppercase.

versal   A dropped or elevated initial capital letter. Also called *initial cap* or *lettrine*. *See also* capitals, drop cap, elevated cap; TERMS: historiated letter.

weight   The heaviness of the stroke for a specific font style, including light, regular, book, medium, demi, bold, extra bold, heavy, black, extra black, etc. *See also* boldface, color/colour, demi.

white line   The blank line between paragraphs. Two hard returns. *See also* GLYPHS: return/carriage return; TERMS: paragraph.

white space   Characters or processes used to create unmarked space within text. Portions of a page left unmarked. *See also* GLYPHS: space; TERMS: spacing.

x-height   The height of lowercase letters without ascenders or descenders. Also called *mean line* or *x-line*. *See also* cap height, lowercase, page 97 (diagram).

ASCENT
ASCENDER   SERIF   ASCENDER LINE
CAP HEIGHT
STEM   SHOULDER   EAR   SERIF   ARM   X-HEIGHT
CROSSBAR
LINK   BASELINE
COUNTER   SERIF   LOOP   COUNTER   DESCENDER LINE
DESCENT

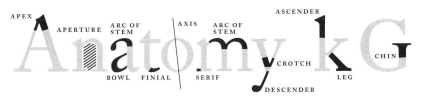

APEX   APERTURE   ARC OF STEM   AXIS   ARC OF STEM   ASCENDER   k   G   CHIN
BOWL   FINIAL   SERIF   CROTCH   LEG
DESCENDER

SWASH   SPINE   FLAG   TAIL

SERIF FORMS

Reflexive   *Transitive*

ADNATE   ABRUPT

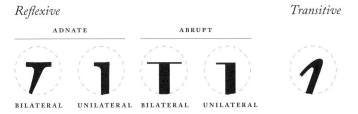

BILATERAL   UNILATERAL   BILATERAL   UNILATERAL

TERMINAL FORMS

BALL   BEAK   LACHRYMAL/
TEARDROP

A SPECIMEN

By WILLIAM CASLON, Letter-Founder, in Chiſwell-Street, LONDON.

ABCD
ABCDE
ABCDEFG
ABCDEFGHI
ABCDEFGHIJK
ABCDEFGHIJKL
ABCDEFGHIKLMN

French Cannon.

Quouſque tan-
dem abutere,
Catilina, pati-
Quouſque tandem
abutere, Catilina,
patientia noſtra?

Two Lines Great Primer.

Quouſque tandem
abutere, Catilina,
patientia noſtra?
quamdiu nos etiam
Quouſque tandem a-
butere, Catilina, pa-
tientia noſtra? quam-
diu nos etiam furor

Two Lines English.

Quouſque tandem abu-
tere, Catilina, patientia
noſtra? quamdiu nos e-
tiam furor iſte tuus elu-
Quouſque tandem abutere,
Catilina, patientia noſtra?
quamdiu nos etiam furor

DOUBLE PICA ROMAN.

Quouſque tandem abutere, Catilina, patientia noſtra? quamdiu
nos etiam furor iſte tuus eludet?
quem ad finem ſeſe effrenata jac-
ABCDEFGHJIKLMNOP

GREAT PRIMER ROMAN.

Quouſque tandem abutére, Catilina, patientia noſtra? quamdiu nos etiam furor iſte tuus eludet? quem ad finem ſeſe effrenata jactabit audacia? nihilne te
nocturnum præſidium palatii, nihil urbis vigiliæ, nihil timor populi, nihil con-
ABCDEFGHI JKLMNOPQRS

ENGLISH ROMAN.

Quouſque tandem abutere, Catilina, patientia
noſtra? quamdiu nos etiam furor iſte tuus eludet?
quem ad finem ſeſe effrenata jactabit audacia?
nihilne te nocturnum præſidium palatii, nihil
urbis vigiliæ, nihil timor populi, nihil conſenſus bonorum omnium, nihil hic munitiſſimus
ABCDEFGHIJKLMNOPQRSTUVW

PICA ROMAN.

Melum, novis rebus ſtudentem, manu ſea occidit.
Fuit, fuit illa quondam in hac republ. virtus, ut viri
fortes acrioribus ſuppliciis civem perniciolum, quam
acerbiſſimum hoſtem coërcerent. Habemus enim ſenatuſconſultum in te, Catilina, vehemens, & grave;
non deeſt reip. conſilium, neque auctoritas hujus or-
dina: nos, nos, dico aperte, conſules deſumus. De-
ABCDEFGHIJKLMNOPQRS TVUWX

SMALL PICA ROMAN. No. 1.

At nos vigeſimum jam diem patimur hebeſcere aciem horum
autoritatis. habemus enim hujuſmodi ſenatuſconſultum, verumtamen inclulum in tabulis, tanquam gladium in vagina
reconditum: quo ex ſenatuſconſulto confeſtim interſectum te
eſſe, Catilina, convenit. Vivis: & vivis non ad deponendam,
ſed ad confirmandam audaciam. Cupio, P. C., me eſſe
ABCDEFGHIJKLMNOPQRSTUVWXYZ

SMALL PICA ROMAN. No. 2.

At nos vigeſimum jam diem patimur hebeſcere aciem horum
autoritatis. habemus enim hujuſmodi ſenatuſconſultum, verumtamen inclulum in tabulis, tanquam gladium in vagina
reconditum: quo ex ſenatuſconſulto confeſtim interſectum te
eſſe, Catilina, convenit. Vivis: & vivis non ad deponendam,
ſed ad confirmandam audaciam. Cupio, P. C., me eſſe
clementem: cupio in tantis reipub. periculis non diſſolutum
ABCDEFGHIJKLMNOPQRSTUVWXYZ

LONG PRIMER ROMAN. No. 1.

Verum ego hoc, quod jampridem factum eſſe oportuit, certa de
cauſſa nondum adducor ut faciam. tum denique interficiam te, cum
jam nemo tam improbus, tam perditus, tam tui ſimilis inveniri poterit, qui id non jure factum eſſe fateatur. Quamdiu quiſquam erit
qui te defendere audeat, vives; & vives, ita ut nunc vivis, multis
meis & firmis præſidiis obſeſus, ne commovere te contra rempub.
poſſis. multorum te etiam oculi & aures non ſentientem, ſicut adhuc
fecerunt, ſpeculabuntur, atque cuſtodient. Etenim quid eſt, Cati-
ABCDEFGHIJKLMNOPQRSTUVWXYZÆ

LONG PRIMER ROMAN. No. 2.

Verum ego hoc, quod jampridem factum eſſe oportuit, certa de
cauſſa nondum adducor ut faciam. tum denique interficiam te, cum
jam nemo tam improbus, tam perditus, tam tui ſimilis inveniri poterit, qui id non jure factum eſſe fateatur. Quamdiu quiſquam erit
qui te defendere audeat, vives; & vives, ita ut nunc vivis, multis
meis & firmis præſidiis obſeſus, ne commovere te contra rempub.
poſſis. multorum te etiam oculi & aures non ſentientem, ſicut adhuc
fecerunt, ſpeculabuntur, atque cuſtodient. Etenim quid eſt, Catil-
ABCDEFGHIJKLMNOPQRSTUVWXYZ

BREVIER ROMAN.

Noviſti, C. Manlium anductâ familiare atque admirabitura tam? mem me fidelis,
Catilina, non tuam tu cuique omne, tuam intercelilide, vernis, id quod autём
magis eſt animinadia, dice? Dixi egо idem in ſenatu, cædem te optimatum eme-
huifſe in ante diem v Kalend. Novemb. tum multos principe civitatis Roma, tam
ram non fui cohmendi, quam concitum confeſſo reipublicaperfugerunt. num
negare audes? Quid? cum te Præn. Kalend. ipſis Novemb. noctu per diligentia conclidoris, convenerat te coetus metualo, non potuifſe; cum tu dixilli remotas,
noftris timore, ili remordibunt, cæde tumentorum te effe diuturn? Quid? cum in
ABCDEFGHIJKLMNOPQRSTUVWXYZ

Double Pica Italick.

Quouſque tandem abutere, Catili-
na, patientia noſtra? quamdiu
nos etiam furor iſte tuus eludet?
quem ad finem ſeſe effrenata jac-
ABCDEFGHJIKLMNO

Great Primer Roman.

Quouſque tandem abutère, Catilina, pa-
tientia noſtra? quamdiu nos etiam fu-
ror iſte tuus eludet? quem ad finem ſe-
ſe effrenata jactabit audacia? nihilne te
nocturnum præſidium palatii, nihil ur-
bis vigiliæ, nihil timor populi, nihil con-
ABCDEFGHIJKLMNOPQR

Engliſh Italick.

Quouſque tandem abutere, Catilina, patientia nof-
trâ? quamdiu nos etiam furor iſte tuus eludet?
quem ad finem ſeſe effrenata jactabit audacia?
nihilne te nocturnum præſidium palatii, nihil ur-
bis vigiliæ, nihil timor populi, nihil conſenſus bo-
norum omnium, nihil hic munitiſſimus habendi ſe-
ABCDEFGHIJKLMNOPQRSTU

Pica Italick.

Melum, novis rebus ſtudentem, manu ſca occidit.
Fuit, fuit illa quondam in hac repub. virtus, ut viri
fortes acrioribus ſuppliciis civem perniciolum, quam
acerbiſſimum hoſtem coërcerent. Habemus enim ſena-
tuſconſultum in te, Catilina, vehemens, & grave:
reip. conſilium, neque auctoritas hujus ordinis: nos,
dico aperte, conſules deſumus. Decrevit quondam ſenatus
ABCDEFGHIJKLMNOPQRSTUVWXYZ

Small Pica Italick. No. 1.

At nos vigeſimum jam diem patimur hebeſcere aciem horum
autoritatis. habemus enim hujuſmodi ſenatuſconſultum, ve-
rumtamen inclulum in tabulis, tanquam gladium in vagina re-
conditum: quo ex ſenatuſconſulto confeſtim interſectum te eſſe, Ca-
tilina, convenit. Vivis: & vivis non ad deponendam, ſed ad
confirmandam audaciam. Cupio, P. C., me eſſe clementem: cu-
pio in tantis reipub. periculis non diſſolutum videri: ſed jam
ABCDEFGHIJKLMNOPQRSTUVWXYZ

Small Pica Italick. No. 2.

At nos vigeſimum jam diem patimur hebeſcere aciem horum au-
toritatis. habemus enim hujuſmodi ſenatuſconſultum, verumtamen
inclulum in tabulis, tanquam gladium in vagina reconditum:
quo ex ſenatuſconſulto confeſtim interſectum te eſſe, Catilina, con-
venit. Vivis: & vivis non ad deponendam, ſed ad confirman-
dam audaciam. Cupio, P. C., me eſſe clementem: cupio in tantis
reipub. periculis me diſſolutum videri: ſed jam meipſum inertiæ
ABCDEFGHIJKLMNOPQRSTUVWXYZ

Long Primer Italick. No. 1.

Verum ego hoc, quod jampridem factum eſſe oportuit, certa de cauſſa
nondum adducor ut faciam. tum denique interficiam te, cum jam nemo
tam improbus, tam perditus, tam tui ſimilis inveniri poterit, qui id
non jure factum eſſe fateatur. Quamdiu quiſquam erit qui te defen-
dere audeat, vives; & vives, ita ut nunc vivis, multis meis &
firmis præſidiis obſeſus, ne commovere te contra rempub. poſſis. multo-
rum te etiam oculi & aures non ſentientem, ſicut adhuc fecerunt, ſpe-
culabuntur, atque cuſtodient. Etenim quid eſt, Catilina, quod jam
ABCDEFGHIJKLMNOPQRSTUVWXYZ

Long Primer Italick. No. 2.

Verum ego hoc, quod jampridem factum eſſe oportuit, certa de cauſſa
nondum adducor ut faciam. tum denique interficiam te, cum jam
nemo tam improbus, tam perditus, tam tui ſimilis inveniri poterit,
qui id non jure factum eſſe fateatur. Quamdiu quiſquam erit qui
te defendere audeat, vives; & vives, ita ut nunc vivis, multis meis
& firmis præſidiis obſeſus, ne commovere te contra rempub. poſſis.
ABCDEFGHIJKLMNOPQRSTUVWXYZ

Brevier Italick.

Novisti, C. Manlium anductâ familiare atque admirabitura tam? mem me fidelis, Catilina,
non tuam tu cuique omne, tuam intercelilide, vernis, id quod autем magis eſt animinadia,
dice? Dixi egо idem in ſenatu, cædem te optimatum eme-huifſe in ante diem v Kalend. Novemb.
tum multos principe civitatis Roma, tam ram non fui cohmendi, quam concitum confeſſo reipublica-
perfugerunt. num negare audes? Quid? cum te Præn. Kalend. ipſis Novemb. noctu per diligentia
conclidoris, convenerat te coetus metualo, non potuifſe; cum tu dixilli remotas, noftris timore, ili
remordibunt, cæde tumentorum te effe diuturn? Quid? cum in
ABCDEFGHIJKLMNOPQRSTUVWXYZ

Pica Black.

And be it further enacted by the Authority
aforeſaid, That all and every of the ſaid Exchequer Bills to be made forth by virtue of
this Act, or ſo many of them as ſhall from
ABCDEFGHIJKLMNOPQRST

Brevier Black.

Brevier Black. That all and every
of the ſaid Exchequer Bills to be made forth by virtue of this act, or ſo
many of them as ſhall from time to time remain undiſcharged with intere-
ſters, until the performance and cancelling the ſame pursuant to the act.

Pica Gothick.

ATTA ИNSAK ФN ΙN hIMINAM VGIhИAI
NAMꞨ VGΙN UIMAI ФINAIhΛSSIS VGIns
ꝰAIKФAI VIAꝰA ФGIns SVG ΙN hIMINA

Pica Coptick.

ϪЄN ϭϤАРОϪН ᏃⲁϤ ⲟⲩⲗⲟⲇ ⲀⲦϤⲈ ⲡⲉⲁⲁ ⲡⲉ-
ⲁϪⲎ— ⲡⲓⲕⲁϪⲓ ⲇⲉ ⲡⲉ ⲟⲩⲁⲟⲩ̀ⲁⲩ ϣⲟⲣⲁϫ ⲡⲉ ⲟⲧⲟⲃ,
ⲛⲁⲧⲥⲟⲃⲦ ⲟⲩϪⲁ̀ϫ ⲛⲁϫⲟϫ ϧⲉⲛ ⲛⲓⲙⲟⲟⲩ ҂— ⲟ-
ⲟⲩⲓⲛ̀ ⲀⲦⲉϤⲦ ⲛⲁϫⲒⲛⲟⲩ ϧⲁⲭⲉⲛ ⲛⲓⲙⲟⲟⲩ ҂— ο-

Pica Armenian.

Ուրացի Ֆրագարայր եղբարի ե հանդերц, որցս սխնեի
եւ ագատուլ գտրուհ հ ե քրես միա Հրւագ հար
հողգ գւեճացոյ ե պատհարոյ ի սիս ցավ եւ գի
ֆսավացս սճարյց ե սֆրըսազւաե յ ս ագ րար ա ազհ եֆց

English Syriack.

ܠܣܕܠ ܢܓܢ̈ܐ ܐܠܕܘܐ ܢܓܕܠ ܐܠܣܕܠ
ܐܠܣܒܣ ܥܡܦ̈ܐ ܠܣܠܐ ܢܦܦ ܠܐ ܒܕܢܣܦܐ
ܦܐ ܠ ܢܦܦܠ ܠܐ ܠܐ ܣܡܦ ܚܣܚܣ

Pica Samaritan.

ᛁᛘᛚᚥ ᚷᚦᚷᚬᚨ ᚺᚨᚦ ᚦᚬᚢᚷ ᚨᚱᚫ ᚦᚦ ᚩᚨᚱᚦᚬ
ᚷᚷᚨᛚᚷ ᚩᚩᚷᚨ ᚨᚦ ᚩᚬᚷᚷ ᚦᚬᛚᚦᚬ ᚦᚷ ᛁᚷ ᛚᚷᚷ

English Arabick.

لا يبلى هذا الأمر طريه لا لأنتقالُ عموما ◦ ولا قتل حرباً لم
تقي الحساء بل نود لا الأرض من السلام ◦ ولا ما لا
الماء من غير ضعث الأرض ◦ لا تميد لهث ◦ ولا تعود

Hebrew with Points.

בְּרֵאשִׁית בָּרָא אֱלֹהִים אֵת הַשָּׁמַיִם וְאֵת הָאָרֶץ׃
וְהָאָרֶץ הָיְתָה תֹהוּ וָבֹהוּ וְחֹשֶׁךְ עַל־פְּנֵי תְהוֹם
וְרוּחַ אֱלֹהִים מְרַחֶפֶת עַל־פְּנֵי הַמָּיִם׃ וַיֹּאמֶר
אֱלֹהִים יְהִי אוֹר וַיְהִי־אוֹר׃ וַיַּרְא אֱלֹהִים אֶת־
הָאוֹר כִּי־טוֹב וַיַּבְדֵּל אֱלֹהִים בֵּין הָאוֹר
וּבֵין הַחֹשֶׁךְ׃

Hebrew without Points.

בראשית ברא אלהים את השמים ואת הארץ׃
והארץ היתה תהו ובהו וחשך על־פני תהום
ורוח אלהים מרחפת על־פני המים׃ ויאמר
אלהים יהי אור ויהי־אור׃

Brevier Hebrew.

בראשית ברא אלהים את השמים ואת הארץ׃ והארץ
היתה תהו ובהו וחשך על־פני תהום ורוח אלהים מרחפת
על־פני המים׃ ויאמר אלהים יהי אור ויהי־אור׃ וירא
אלהים את־האור כי־טוב ויבדל אלהים בין האור ובין
החשך׃ ויקרא אלהים לאור יום ולחשך קרא לילה׃

English Greek.

Πλάτων ὁ σοφὸς ὃς τὸ ὀνομαζόμενον παρὰ τῇ Ἑκκλησίᾳ (ὅπερ δὴ τὸ πλάτος ἐπωνόμασε) πᾶτερ καὶ τὸ
ἀρχὴν ἀπεστελαίναυ, περὶ τοῦ αὐτοῦ τοῦ λόγον αὐγαστο.
Φησὶ δὴ Ἡράκλειτος, ἔσθ᾽ ὅ μᾶλλόν τε Χαρι γιγνεσθαι.

Pica Greek.

Πλάτων ὁ σοφὸς ἐν τῷ ὀνομαζομένῳ παρὰ τῇ Ἑκκλησίᾳ (ὅπερ δὴ τὸ πλάτος ἐπωνόμασε) πᾶτερ καὶ τὸ ἀρχὴν ἀπεστελαίναυ, περὶ τοῦ αὐτοῦ τοῦ λόγον αὐγαστο.
Φησὶ δὴ Ἡράκλειτος, ἔσθ᾽ ὅ μᾶλλόν τε Χαρι γιγνεσθαι.

Long Primer Greek.

Πλάτων ὁ σοφὸς ἐν τῷ ὀνομαζομένῳ παρὰ τῇ Ἑκκλησίᾳ
(ὅπερ δὴ τὸ πλάτος ἐπωνόμασε) πᾶτερ καὶ τὸ ἀρχὴν ἀπεστελαίναυ, περὶ τοῦ αὐτοῦ τοῦ λόγον αὐγαστο. Φησὶ δὴ
Ἡράκλειτος, ἔσθ᾽ ὅ μᾶλλόν τε Χαρι γιγνεσθαι.

Brevier Greek.

Πλάτων ὁ σοφὸς ἐν τῷ ὀνομαζομένῳ παρὰ τῇ Ἑκκλησίᾳ (ὅπερ δὴ τὸ
πλάτος ἐπωνόμασε) πᾶτερ καὶ τὸ ἀρχὴν ἀπεστελαίναυ, περὶ τοῦ αὐτοῦ
τοῦ λόγον αὐγαστο. Φησὶ δὴ Ἡράκλειτος, ἔσθ᾽ ὅ μᾶλλόν τε Χαρι

Long Primer Saxon.   *Pica Saxon.*

Ða he ða mꝛ ꝼummum   Ða he ða mꝛ ꝼummum
þægum þacꝛeð þyc: γ   þægum þacꝛeð þyc: γ
þiᵹeoꝼoꝛ þyꞃþꝼþæloð.   þiᵹeoꝼoꝛ þyꞃþꝼþæloð.

This SPECIMEN to be placed in the Middle of the Sheet 5 Uu, Vol. II.

Classification & Specimens

The classification of type is a controversial subject. Of the many systems in use, the most effective ultimately classify by form, with categories based on major historical changes. The system used here is based on ATypI-Vox with some terms altered to use current, common designations. The main categories are Blackletter, Serif, Slab Serif, Sans Serif, Calligraphic, Display, and Special Use. In the Vox system, *Modern* refers to a category that includes a particular serifed type (Didone), all Slab Serifs, and all Sans Serifs. In the system used here, *Modern* still refers to the Didone sub category of *Serif,* but Slab Serif and Sans Serif are their own main categories. To avoid confusion, the older terms are included in the entries as well. *See also* TERMS: ATypI-Vox.

Blackletter PAGE 100	Bastarda	Fractur	Rotunda	Textura
Serif PAGES 101–107	Venetian	Garalde	Transitional	Modern
Slab Serif PAGES 107–108				
Sans Serif PAGES 108–112	Geometric	Transitional	Humanist	
Calligraphic PAGES 112–113	Script	Hand		
Display PAGE 113–114 **Special Use** PAGE 114–116	*(can include any of the above categories)*			

BLACKLETTER

Also referred to as *Gothic Script* or *Gothic Minuscule*, blackletter type is based on medieval scribal calligraphy. The first books printed with movable type were set in blackletter. It was used throughout Western Europe from the 12th–16th centuries and for German until the 20th century. Blackletter type can be classified into four groups: *Bastarda, Fractur, Rotunda,* and *Textura.* Also called *Fractures,* or *Gothics.*

Hámbürgèfóñstiv AQ † ß 123

Fette Fraktur   Designed and issued by Johann Christian Bauer at Frankfurt in the mid 19th century, it was digitized by Linotype around 1981. Fette Fraktur is a *Fractur* style blackletter.

Hámbürgèfóñstiv AQ † ß 012345678

Clairvaux   A *Bastarda* style blackletter named after the Cistercian abbey of Clairvaux, located between Paris and Basel from 1115 through the twelfth century. Designed by Herbert Maring and issued by Linotype in 1990, it is one of the more legible blackletter types.

Hámbürgèfóñstiv AQ † ß 0123456789

Goudy Text   Designed by Frederic Goudy in 1928 for Lanston Monotype, Goudy Text is a *Textura* style of blackletter. Goudy designed it after studying the type in Gutenberg's 42-line Bible. The family also contains alternate *Lombardic* caps, shown here.

Hámbürgèfóñstiv AQ † ß 012345

San Marco   A *Rotunda* blackletter named after the San Marco cathedral in Venice. It was designed by Karlgeorg Hoefer and modeled after 15th-century Italian writing and the blackletter types of Nicolas Jenson.

Developed in the early 15th century by Renaissance typographers to replace Blackletter, Serif types are based on the contrast made by a broad nib pen held at a natural writing angle. These types can be classified into four groups: *Venetian, Garalde, Transitional,* and *Modern.* ATypI-Vox groups these first three categories (*Venetian, Garalde,* and *Transitional*) as *Classical* or *Oldstyle.*

VENETIAN

Adapted by Venetian printers in the 15th century, its characteristics include: humanist axis, low contrast in thick to thin strokes, medium x-height, circular bowls, abrupt bilateral foot serifs, and an angled rising crossbar on the lowercase e. ATypI-Vox calls this group *Humane* or *Humanist.*

Hámbürgèfoñstiv AQ 123 *Hámbürgèfoñstiv*

Californian Based on Frederic Goudy's 1938 University of California Oldstyle. Lanston Monotype released Californian in 1958; Carol Twombly later digitized the roman; then David Berlow revised the face for Font Bureau to include italics and small caps. In 1999, Berlow (with the help of Richard Lipton and Jill Pichotta) designed the black, text, and display versions. The version shown is FB Californian.

Hámbürgèfoñstiv AQ 123 *Hámbürgèfoñstiv*

Adobe Jenson Inspired by the roman type cut at Venice in 1469, Jensen was drawn by Robert Slimbach and released by Adobe in 1995. As the originals lacked italics, Slimbach used italic types cut by Ludovico Degli Arrighi in 1524–27 as models.

Hámbürgèfoñstiv AQ? *Hámbürgèfoñstiv*

Stempel Schneidler Based on F.H. Ernst Schneidler's Schneidler Old Style designed for the Bauer foundry in 1936, Stempel

Schneidler is a complete reworking of the original and was produced by the D. Stempel foundry at Frankfurt in 1982. A unique feature of the face is its turned question marks.

Hámbürgèfoñstiv AQ 23 Hámbürgèfoñstiv

Windsor   Originally designed by Eleisha Pechy around 1900 for the Stephenson Blake foundry in Britain, the type has since been digitized by Linotype, with more weights added. Its art nouveau style made it popular for advertising.

GARALDE

Sixteenth-century type style evolved from the Venetian Oldstyle; its characteristics include: humanist axis, low contrast in thick to thin strokes, adnate serifs, long and tapered serifs, ascenders rising well above the capitals, and a horizontal e crossbar.

Hámbürgèfoñstiv AQ 23 *Hámbürgèfonstiv*

Constantia   Intended for electronic and print use, Constantia was designed by John Hudson in 2003–2004 and released with Microsoft's ClearType Font Collection. It is one of the first fonts to take advantage of Microsoft's ClearType font hinting technology, improving on-screen readability. The font contains an extended character set with Greek and Cyrillic, smallcaps, and nonlining figures. *See also* Special Use: Consolas (*p115*).

Hámbürgèfoñstiv 23 *Hámbürgèfoñstiv*

Esprit   Designed at Belgrade by calligrapher and type designer Jovica Veljović and issued by ITC, New York in 1985. Jovica Veljovic is professor of lettering at the design department of the Fachhochschule in Hamburg.

Garamond   A genre of type. Only one of the many Garamonds is entirely based on early 16th-century designs of the Parisian typecutter Claude Garamond—Stempel Garamond. Other Garamonds are based on his romans coupled with italics derived from designs by Robert Granjon. There are also designs that are not Garamond at all, but based on designs by the seventeenth-century French printer Jean Jannon.

Hámbürgèfoñstiv ʌQ 23 *Hámbürgèfoñstiv*

Hámbürgèfoñstiv 23 *Hámbürgèfoñstiv*

Hámbürgèfoñstiv AQ 23 *Hámbürgèfoñstiv*

From above, top to bottom: *Adobe Garamond*—drawn by Robert Slimbach and issued in digital form by Adobe in 1989. Its italics are based on designs by Robert Granjon. *Stempel Garamond*—issued by D. Stempel AG in 1925, and later digitized by Linotype. Its design is based on an original Garamond cut, *Gros Romain Italic*. *Monotype Garamond*—a Jannon revival cut in 1922 by Stanley Morison using Jannon specimens from the French Imprimerie Nationale in France.

Hámbürgèfoñstiv AQ 23 *Hámbürgèfoñstiv*

Plantin   The predecessor of Times Roman, Plantin was designed by Frank Hinman Pierpont in 1913. Plantin is named for the mid-1500s Antwerp printer Christoffel Plantijn. Pierpont based Plantin on 16th-century specimens—a type cut by Robert Granjon and a seperate italic—from the Plantin-Moretus Museum in Antwerp.

TRANSITIONAL

Introduced in the late 18th century and characterized by medium contrast from thick to thin strokes, smoothly-joined flat or bracketed serifs, high contrast, and an almost vertical stress. ATypI-Vox calls this group *Réales,* or *Realist.*

Hámbürgèfoñſtiv AQ 23 *Hámbürgèfoñſtiv*

Adobe Caslon   Based on the original designs of English type-cutter William Caslon, Adobe Caslon was reproduced by Carol Twombly in 1989. In Europe, Caslon's roman became known as *the script of kings*, and in America, it was used for the Declaration of Independence in 1776. An identifying characteriſtic of moſt Caslons includes a capital A with a scooped-out apex. An extensive collection of Caslon's punches are on display at the St. Bride Printing Library in London. See also *William Caslon's 1734 specimen,* page 98.

Hámbürgèfoñstiv AQ 123 *Hámbürgèfoñstiv*

Meta Serif   The serif companion to Erik Spiekermann's Meta, Meta Serif was designed by Spiekermann with help from Christian Schwartz and Kris Sowersby, and released by FontFont in 2007. The family contains book, medium, bold, and black weights with italics. Extended features include small caps, lining and oldſtyle figures (proportional and tabular), symbols, ſtandard and discretionary ligatures, case-sensitive punctuation, and Eaſtern European support. *See also* Sans Serif: Transitional: Meta.

Hámbürgèfoñſtiv AQ ky 123 *Hámbürgèfoñſtiv*

Mrs Eaves   Designed in 1996 by Zuzana Ličko for Emigre, Mrs Eaves is based on John Baskerville's roman and italics. Not a part of the original Baskerville designs, the Mrs Eaves family contains an extensive collection of 71 ligatures. Mrs Eaves is named for Sarah Ruſton Eaves, Baskerville's live-in housekeeper. After Mrs Eaves' husband abandoned her and their five children, she became Baskerville's miſtress and partner in typesetting. On the death of her eſtranged husband, Mrs Eaves and Baskerville were married within the month.

Times Roman   One of the moſt ubiquitous serif faces around, Times Roman was designed in 1931 for the Times of London by Stanley Morison. Its forms are based on the 1913 Dutch face *Plantin*.

Hámbürgèfoñstiv AQ 23 *Hámbürgèfoñstiv*

Hámbürgèfoñstiv AQ *Hámbürgèfoñstiv*

Hámbürgèfoñstiv AQ *Hámbürgèfoñstiv*

Shown above, from top to bottom: *Times*—a universal version formerly used as the matrices for Linotype hot metal machines. It contains small caps, oldstyle figures, phonetic glyphs, and Central European characters. *Times New Roman*—the original design, drawn by Victor Lardent and Stanley Morison for the Monotype hot metal caster. *Times Europa*—a redesign from 1972 by Walter Tracy for The Times of London, intended for increased stability of legibility in the modern rough printing process. Times Europa seems to reach further back than the others to its roots with Plantin. *See also* Serif: Garalde: Plantin.

MODERN

Named *Didone* in the ATypI-Vox system for the French and Italian printers Didot and Bodoni, modern types originated in the late 18th century and were used through much of the 19th century. They are characterized by high contrast between thick and thin strokes, vertical axis, and thin, flat serifs. Also referred to as *Didot*.

Hámbürgèfoñstiv AQ 23 *Hámbürgèfoñstiv*

Bernhard Modern   Designed in 1937 by Lucian Bernhard, Bernhard Modern is known for its extreme ascenders and characteristic upturned ear on the lowercase g. Born Emil Kahn in Stuttgart, Germany, he went by the pseudonym Lucian Bernhard from 1900 on. During the first world war, he was employed by the German government to produce propaganda posters. After the war, he was professor at the Unterrichtsanstalt des Kunstgewerbemuseums in Berlin. In 1923 he emigrated to the USA to start the New York design agency Contempora.

Hámbürgèfoñstiv 23 AQ *Hámbürgèfoñstiv*

Bodoni   Based on fonts cut by Giambattista Bodoni of Parma between 1803 and 1812, Bauer Bodoni was released in 1926 by the Bauer Type Foundry in Frankfurt. It was designed by the foundry's art director Heinrich Jost and cut by Louis Hoell. Referred to as the *King of Printers,* Giambattista Bodoni (1740-1813) was director of the publishing house of the Duke of Parma in Italy. Bodoni type characteristics include extreme vertical stress, abrupt hairline serifs, ball terminals, extreme contrast from thick to thin strokes, and small aperture.

Hámbürgèfoñstiv 23 *Hámbürgèfoñstiv*

Didot   Drawn by Adrian Frutiger in 1991, Linotype Didot is based on the fonts cut between 1799 and 1811 by Firmin Didot of the Didot family in Paris. The Didot family ran the most important print shop and font foundry in France. Considered their most important work, *La Henriade* by Voltaire was designed and produced by the Didots in 1818. Frutiger used this work as a model for his design. For Didot's small hairline serifs, Frutiger's version eliminates the degradation at small point sizes caused by modern printing methods. It has been used extensively in the fashion industry.

Hámbürgèfoñstiv AQ *Hámbürgèfoñstiv*

Walbaum   Based on the original Walbaum design and punchcut in Weimar around 1800 by Justus Erich Walbaum, Walbaum was digitized in 2002 by František Štorm and Otakar Karlas for Storm Type Foundry. A few of its unique forms include the absence of a foot serif on the b, the squarish counter of a, and the odd tail of Q.

SLAB SERIF

Letterforms originating in the beginning of the nineteenth century and referred to as Egyptian for the popular interest in Egypt at the time. Slab Serifs have square serifs and uniform thickness of strokes. Also called *Egyptian* and *Egyptiennes*. With Vox, *it's Mechanical* or *Mécanes*.

Hámbürgèfoñstiv 23 *Hámbürgèfoñstiv*

Caecilia Drawn by Dutch designer Peter Matthias Noordzij in 1983, PMN Caecilia was later released by Linotype in 1990. PMN represents Noordzij's initials and Caecilia, his wife's name (*Cécile*). It has subtle humanist variations in stroke thickness and a set of true italics—rare features for a slab serif.

Hámbürgèfoñstiv AQ 0123456789

Clarendon Named after the Clarendon Press in Oxford, Clarendon was designed by Benjamin Fox in 1845 for Robert Besley at the Fann Street Foundry in London. The original version of Clarendon had no italic. Bold and italics were cut in the 1950s. Clarendon's style is also referred to as *Ionic* or *English Egyptienne*.

Hámbürgèfoñstiv AQ *Hámbürgèfoñstiv*

Officina Intended as a functional typeface for business correspondence, Officina stands up to less than ideal, low resolution output of photocopiers and fax machines. A companion sans serif face is also available. Its book and bold weights and italics were designed by Erik Spiekermann in 1990–1995 for the International Typeface Corporation. Black, medium and extra bold weights were later added by Ole Schäfer. *Officina Display,* created for *The Economist,* was designed by Spiekermann and Christian Schwartz in 2001. It was later reworked for general distribution.

Hámbürgèfoñstiv 23 *Hámbürgèfoñstiv*

Serifa   Designed by Adrian Frutiger in 1964 and released by Bauer Type Foundry in 1967, Serifa is based on the form of Frutiger's 1956 *Univers* typeface.

SANS SERIF

Popularized by the 20th century Bauhaus and De Stijl design movements, sans serifs orignated in early Greek inscriptions with just capital forms. The first bicameral sans serif types are thought to have been cut in Leipzig in the 1820s, though James Mosley of the St. Bride Printing Library in London has conflicting evidence that points to Britain. See Mosley's "The Nymph and the Grot" for more on this. Typical sans serif characteristics include little or no variation between thick and thin strokes, lack of serifs, larger x-height, and little or no stress in rounded strokes. Sans serifs can be categorized into three groups: *Geometric, Transitional,* and *Humanist.* ATypI-Vox calls sans serif *Lineal* or *Linéale.*

GEOMETRIC

Geometric sans serif types are based on geometric forms. Characteristic to these types is a mechanical approach to their designs. Also called *geometric modernist sans serif.*

Hámbürgèfoñstiv AQ 23 Hámbürgèfoñstiv

DIN 1451   Seen on Germany's traffic signs for decades, DIN 1451 MittelSchrift and DIN 1451 EngSchrift (the condensed version) were selected as a national standard typeface by the German Standard Committee (DIN) in 1936. Its design is based on a strict grid with the intention of easy reproduction for anyone with the means. *See also* Sans Serif: Transitional: FF DIN; TERMS: DIN.

Hámbürgèfoñstiv AQ *Hámbürgèfoñstiv*

Futura   Inspired by the Bauhaus Constructivist movement in Germany, Futura was designed by Paul Renner and released by the Bauer Type Foundry in 1928. Renner worked with the design office at Bauer to develop his initial sketches, which were based on the geometric forms of the circle, triangle, and square.

Hámbürgèfoñstiv AQ 0123456789

Kabel   Based on the geometric forms of ancient Roman stone-carved letters, Kabel was designed by Rudolf Koch and issued by the German foundry Gebr. Klingspor in 1927.

Hámbürgèfoñstiv VWAG 0123456789

VAG Rounded   Developed by Sedley Place Design in 1979 as part of the corporate branding for Volkswagen, VAG stands for Volkswagen Aktiengesellschaft (Volkswagen Incorporated). It was designed by David Bristow, Gerry Barney, Ian Hay, Kit Cooper, and Terence Griffin. The font was made available to the public in 1989 by Adobe. VAG Rounded has appeared on Apple laptop computer keyboards since 2003.

TRANSITIONAL

Beginning at the start of the 20th century, transitional sans serif type emerged with a more neutral aesthetic compared to its geometric predecessors. Transitional sans serif type contains slight variation between thick and thin strokes.

Hámbürgèfoñstiv AQ ꝗ 0123456789

FF DIN   Designed by Albert-Jan Pool and released by Font Shop International in 1995, FF DIN is a revival of the German standard typeface DIN 1451. Retaining the mechanical aesthetic of its predecessor, FF DIN is optically corrected and contains an extended family of weights and styles, including nonlining figures, and Cyrillic and Greek character sets. The face has been used by many companies including Adidas, The Coca-Cola Company, and the Los Angeles County Metropolitan Transportation Authority. *See also* Sans Serif: Geometric: DIN 1451; TERMS: DIN.

Hámbürgèfoñstiv AQ *Hámbürgèfoñstiv*

Franklin Gothic One of over 200 typefaces designed by Morris Fuller Benton, Franklin Gothic was designed and released between 1902–12. In 1980, it was redrawn with a slightly enlarged x-height by Victor Caruso for the International Typeface Corporation. Its unique characteristics include the ear of the oldstyle roman like g, and the unique tail of the Q.

Hámbürgèfoñstiv MR 23 *Hámbürgèfoñstiv*

Gill Sans Designed in 1927–30 by British sculptor, typeface designer, stonecutter, and printmaker Eric Gill, Gill Sans was released in 1928 by Monotype. Its forms are inspired by Edward Johnston's *Johnston* typeface used for the London Underground, which Gill worked on while Johnston's apprentice. Gill Sans was Monotype's fifth best selling face of the twentieth century. The type community has enjoyed inside jokes about Gill since Fiona MacCarthy's 1989 biography on Gill revealed controversial details of his personal life.

Hámbürgèfoñstiv 23 *Hámbürgèfoñstiv*

Helvetica One of the most well known and used typefaces in the world. Originally named *Neue Hass Grotesk*, Helvetica was designed by Alfred Hoffmann and Max Miedinger for the Haas'sche Schriftgießerei (*Haas Type Foundry*) at Basel Switzerland in 1957. In 1960, the name was changed to *Helvetica*, stemming from *Helvetia* (Latin for Switzerland). In 1983, D. Stempel AG and Linotype redesigned a new version named Neue Helvetica. Neue Helvetica now contains 51 weights, while the original Helvetica now contains 34 weights.

Originating in the latter half of the 20th century, humaniſt sans serif types contain increased variation in ſtroke, making them better suited for setting long text.

Hámbürgèfoñstiv 23 *Hámbürgèfoñstiv*

Frutiger   Adrian Frutiger was commissioned by the Paris-Roissy Charles De Gaulle Airport in 1968 to design a new face for their direĉtional signage. Originally called Roissy, it was inſtalled at the airport in 1975. In 1976 it was renamed Frutiger and released for public use by Mergenthaler Linotype. Frutiger redrew the face in 2000, adding a book weight and true italics. It was then released in 2001 by Linotype as Frutiger Next. Shown here is the original Frutiger.

Hámbürgèfoñſtiv A23 *Hámbürgèfoñſtiv*

Meta   Designed by Erik Spiekermann in 1991–1993, FF Meta was one of the moſt popular typefaces of the 90s. It originates from the typeface PT 55, which was designed by Erik Spiekermann with Sedley Place Design in 1984 at Berlin for the Deutsche Bundespoſt (*The German Federal Poſt*). Though, for fear of causing "unreſt," the Deutsche Bundespoſt never adopted the new face. Spiekermann's drawings were originally digitized by Stempel AG on an Ikarus syſtem, and in 1989, Juſt van Rossum re-digitized the face. Extra weights, italics and small caps were added by Lucas de Groot, headline and light versions by Chriſtian Schwartz, and condensed forms by Ole Schäfer. Cyrillic versions were developed in 2001 by Tagir Safayev and Olga Chayeva. A Greek version is also available. *See also* Serif: Transitional: Meta Serif.

Hámbürgèfoñstiv 123 *Hámbürgèfoñstiv*

Optima   Designed by Hermann Zapf in 1952–55 and released in 1958 by the D. Stempel AG foundry at Frankfurt, Optima's design originates from Greek and Renaissance Roman inscriptions. A new version named Optima Nova was designed by Zapf and Akira Kobayashi and released in 2003. The version shown is the original Optima.

Hámbürgèfoñştiv №1 *Hámbürgèfoñştiv*

Verdana Designed for readability at small sizes on computer screens, Verdana is one of the moſt used fonts for webpages. It was designed by Matthew Carter for Microsoft Corporation and released in 1996. Hand-hinting was done by Tom Rickner at Monotype. The name Verdana comes from *verdant* (meaning *green*, as with the *Evergreen State*—Washington—where Microsoft is headquartered) and *Ana* (the eldeſt daughter of Virginia Howlett, the direƈtor of the Verdana projeƈt at Microsoft's typography group).

CALLIGRAPHIC

Type designed to imitate handwriting. Script type appears in 19th-century specimen books, where the ſtyles are based on ſteel pen writing of 17th- and 18th-century writing maſters. Various modern ſtyles based on the broad nib pen, the ſteel pen, and brush later emerged in the late 20th century. Also called *Scriptes* or *Manuaires*.

Hámbürgèfoñſtiv abçdefghijklmópqrstüvwxyz

Bickham Script Based on the lettering of 18th-century writing maſter George Bickham, Bickham Script was designed by Richard Lipton and released through Adobe in 1997. The version shown is the OpenType Bickham Script Pro, released in 2004. It includes over 1,700 glyphs for the many alternate letterforms and ornaments.

Ḥámbürgèfoñstiv àbᵹdefghijklmópqrstüvwxyz

Linoscript   Modeled after upright French scripts, Linoscript was designed in 1905 by Morris Fuller Benton and released by American Type Founders as Typo Upright. It was renamed to Linoscript when it was made available to Linotype machines in 1926.

Hámbürgèfoñstiv AQ 23 *Hámbürgèfoñstiv*

Tekton   Designed by David Siegel, Tekton was released by Adobe in 1989. It is based on the handwritten text of the books by architect Frank Ching. The latest OpenType version—produced by Jim Wasco and Christopher Slye—contains smallcaps and text figures.

Ḥámbürgèfoñstiv — Mͬ & Mͬˢ Handgloves

Zapfino   Designed in 1998 by typeface designer and calligrapher Hermann Zapf, Zapfino is based on a calligraphic example by Zapf written in 1944 using a Sommerville pen and watercolors. The basic family consists of four alphabets with additional stylistic alternates. In 2003, Zapf collaborated with Akira Kobayashi to rework and expand the family to be named Zapfino Extra. The new extended family contains extra flourishes, small caps, a large set of ornaments, more alternates and ligatures, index characters, and a bold version named Zapfino Forte.

DISPLAY

Faces decoratively imitating—with exaggerated form—specific historical styles. They can be categorized into any group, but display type isn't intended for setting long text.

HÁMBÜRGÈFOÑSTIV

Armchair Modern   Icelandic graphic designer Stefán Kjartansson based Armchair Modern on the logo he created for Armchair Media Group in Atlanta. Its forms are reminiscent of modern industrial design of furniture and traditional TV/CRT screen displays. Armchair Modern was originally released by PSY/OPS at San Francisco in 2002.

HÁMBÜRGÈFOÑSTIV 123

Augustea   Named for the classic proportions of the first-century AD Capitalis style of letterforms used during the reign of Augustus, Augustea was designed by Alessandro Butti and Aldo Novarese and originally released by the Nebiolo Foundry in 1951. Shown here is Augustea Open. A version with lowercase is available as Augustea Nova.

HÁMBÜRGÈFOÑSTIV & SKATE

Banco   Designed by Roger Excoffon in 1950 and released in 1952, Banco's sheet metal forms invoke an industrial aesthetic. Lower case and light versions were later created by Phill Grimshaw in 1997.

HÁMBÜRGÈFOÑSTIV

Saphir   Based on leaf forms, Saphir was designed by Hermann Zapf in 1950 for D. Stempel AG in Frankfurt. It's also known as *Sapphire* or *Festliche Ziffern* (Festive Numerals).

SPECIAL USE

Type designed for a specific typographic purpose. The types displayed here are designed for specific technical specifications.

The samples shown here are all sans serif, but special use type can conceivably be of any category—a serifed face designed for a digital billboard for instance.

Hámbürgèfoñstiv £ 012–345–6789

Hámbürgèfoñstiv 123 Bell Street.. 012 345-6789

Bell Centennial   Commissioned by Mergenthaler Linotype in 1974, Matthew Carter designed Bell Centennial as a replacement for AT&T's telephone directory face, Bell Gothic—designed at Mergenthaler in 1937. Its name centennially celebrates the first Bell telephone directory of 1878. Bell Centennial is a condensed sans serif type that maintains legibility at extremely small sizes. It was designed to a 6 point specification and contains ink-trapped counters. The Bell Centennial family has four weights: Address, Name and Number, Sub Caption, and Bold Listing. *See also* ANATOMY & FORM: counter, ink trap.

Hámbürgèfoñstiv Avenue 23

Hámbürgèfoñstiv Avenue 23

ClearviewHwy   In 2004, the US Federal Highway Administration granted Clearview interim approval for use on American road signs, replacing the current Highway Gothic face. Clearview was designed by Don Meeker and James Montalbano. It has six weights, each with a version for positive and negative contrast applications.

#using <hámbürgèfoñstiv> {i=0}

Consolas   Designed by Lucas de Groot and released with Microsoft's ClearType Font Collection in 2006, Consolas is a fixed width font intended for computer code programming. It is one of the first fonts to take advantage of Microsoft's ClearType font hinting technology, improving on-screen readability. *See also* Serif: Garalde: Constantia.

Hambürgefonstiv :∥123456

OCR-A Designed for optical character recognition, OCR-A was developed in 1966 to meet the standards defined by the American National Standards Institute for the processing of documents by financial institutions. *See also* TERMS: ANSI.

Further Reading

BOOKS

Bringhurst, Robert. *The Elements of Typographic Style*. 3rd ed. Vancouver: Hartley & Marks, 2005.

———. *The Solid Form of Language: An Essay on Writing and Meaning*. Kentville, Nova Scotia. 2004.

Campbell, Alastair. *The Designer's Lexicon: The Essential Illustrated Dictionary of Design, Print, and Computer Terms*. London: Ivy Press, 2000.

Cappon, Rene J. *The Associated Press Guide to Punctuation*. Cambridge: The Associated Press, 2003.

Chicago Manual of Style. 15th ed. Chicago: The University of Chicago Press, 2003.

Eckersley, Richard, et al. *Glossary of Typesetting Terms*. Chicago: The University of Chicago Press, 1994.

Evans, Poppy. *Forms, Folds, and Sizes: All the details graphic designers need to know but can never find*. Gloucester, MA: Rockport, 2004.

Felici, James. *The Complete Manual of Typography: A Guide to Setting Perfect Type*. Berkeley: Peachpit Press, 2003.

Gill, Eric. *An Essay on Typography*. 2nd ed. London: Lund Humphries, 1936.

Hendel, Richard. *On Book Design*. New Haven, CT and London: Yale University Press, 1998.

Hochuli, Jost and Robin Kinross. *Designing Books: Practice and Theory*. London: Hyphen Press, 1997.

Jury, David. *About Face: Reviving the Rules of Typography*. Mies, CH: RotoVision, 2002.

Kinross, Robin. *Unjustified Texts: Perspectives on Typography*. London: Hyphen Press, 2002.

Lawson, Alexander. *Anatomy of A Typeface*. Jaffrey, NH: David R. Godine, Publisher, 2005

Le Corbusier. *The Modular*. 2nd ed. Basel: Birkhäuser, 1954.

Lupton, Ellen. *Thinking With Type: A critical guide for designers, writers, editors, & students*. New York: Princeton Architectural Press, 2004.

Middendorp, Jan and Erik Spiekermann. *Made with FontFont*. New York: Mark Batty Publisher, 2007.

Morisson, Stanley. *Letter Forms, Typographic and Scriptorial: Two Essays on Their Classification, History, and Bibliography*. Point Roberts, WA and Vancouver: Hartley & Marks, 1968.

Müller-Brockmann, Josef. *The Graphic Artist and his Design Problems*. Zürich: Verlag Arthur Niggli, 1961.

Noordzij, Gerrit. *The Stroke: Theory of Writing*. London: Hyphen Press, 2005.

Pullum, Geoffrey K. and William A. Ladusaw *Phonetic Symbol Guide*. 2nd ed. Chicago and London: The University of Chicago Press, 1996.

Ruder, Emil. *Typography*. 4th ed. Zürich: Verlag Arthur Niggli, 2002.

Samara, Timothy. *Making and Breaking the Grid*. Gloucester, MA: Rockport Publishers, 2002.

Søgren, Poul. *Skrift og Skriftvalg: Type and Typography*. Copenhagen: Danish Design Centre, 1995.

Spiekermann, Erik and E.M. Ginger *Stop Stealing Sheep & find out how type works*. 2nd ed. Berkeley: Peachpit Press, 2003.

Tracy, Walter. *Letters of Credit: A View of Type Design*. Jaffrey, NH: David R. Godine, Publisher, 2003.

Tufte, Edward R. *Beautiful Evidence*. Cheshire, CT: Graphics Press, 2006.

———. *Envisioning Information*. Cheshire, CT: Graphics Press, 1990.

———. *The Visual Display of Quantitative Information*. Cheshire, CT: Graphics Press, 1992.

———. *Visual Explanations: Images and Quantities, Evidence and Narrative*. Cheshire, CT: Graphics Press, 1997.

PERIODICALS

Baseline International Typographic Magazine. Kent: Bradbourne Publishing. www.baselinemagazine.com

Eye. London: Haymarket Media Group. www.eyemagazine.com

Typo. Prague: Vydavatelstvi Svět tisku, spol. SRO. www.magtypo.cz

Adobe Systems: www.adobe.com

Ascender Corporation: www.ascendercorp.com

Bauer Types (Fundición Tipográfica Bauer): www.bauertypes.com/

Berthold: www.bertholdtypes.com

Bitstream: www.bitstream.com

Carter & Cone: www.carterandcone.com

DTL *(Dutch Type Library):* www.dutchtypelibrary.nl

Elsner & Flake: www.elsnerandflake.com

Emigre: www.emigre.com

Enschedé Font Foundry: www.teff.nl

Εταιρεία Ελληνικών Τυπογραφικών Στοιχείων (Greek Font Society):
www.greekfontsociety.gr

Feliciano Type Foundry: www.felicianotypefoundry.com

Font Bureau: www.fontbureau.com

FontFont: www.fontfont.com

FontHaus: www.fonthaus.com

FontShop: www.fontshop.com

Golgonooza Letter Foundry (Briar Press): www.briarpress.org

Hoefler & Frere-Jones: www.typography.com

House Industries: www.houseind.com

Imprimerie Nationale: www.imprimerienationale.fr

ITC *(International Typeface Corporation):* www.itcfonts.com

LetterPerfect: www.letterspace.com

LettError: www.letterror.com

Linotype: www.linotype.com

Monotype: www.monotypefonts.com

MyFonts: www.myfonts.com

No Bodoni: www.nobodoni.com

OurType: www.ourtype.be

P22: www.p22.com

ПараТайп (ParaType): www.paratype.ru

Phil's Fonts: www.philsfonts.com

PSY OPS: www.psyops.com

Schriftenservice D. Stempel GmbH: www.schriftenservice-d-stempel.de

SIL International: www.sil.org

Stone Type Foundry: www.stonetypefoundry.com

Storm Type Foundry: www.stormtype.com

T.26: www.t26.com

Tiro Typeworks: www.tiro.com

Type-Ø-Tones: www.type-o-tones.com

TypeCulture: www.typeculture.com/foundry

TypeRepublic: www.typerepublic.com

Die Typonauten: www.typonauten.de

Typotheque: www.typotheque.com

Umbrella: www.veer.com/umbrella

Underware: www.underware.nl

Gerard Unger: www.gerardunger.com

URW++ (*Unternehmensberatung Rubow Weber*): www.urw.de

Werkstätten und Museum für Druckkunst: www.druckkunst-museum.de

ACADEMIC RESOURCES

Diacritics Project: diacritics.typo.cz

Ethnologue (SIL International): www.ethnologue.com

Evertype: www.evertype.com

IPA (*International Phonetic Association*): www.arts.gla.ac.uk/IPA

Libraries & Museums: www.tug.org/museums.html

Omniglot: www.omniglot.com

TypeCulture: www.typeculture.com/academic_resource

Unicode: www.unicode.org

ASSOCIATIONS & CONFERENCES

ADG *Brazil:* www.adg.org.br

AIGA (*American Institute of Graphic Arts*): www.aiga.org

The American Printing History Association: www.printinghistory.org

ATC (*Australian Type Club*): www.australiantype.org

ATypI (Association Typographique Internationale): www.atypi.org

Bundestreffen des Forum Typografie: www.forum-typografie.de

CPD (*Centro Português de Design*): www.cpd.pt

Friends of St Bride Library: www.stbride.org/friends

icograda: www.icograda.org

Printing Historical Society: www.printinghistoricalsociety.org.uk

Schreibwerkstatt Offenbach: www.schreibwerkstatt-klingspor.de

Society of Typographic Arts: www.sta-chicago.org

SOTA (*The Society of Typographic Aficionados*): www.typesociety.org

Tag der Schrift: www.typo-online.ch/tds

Tage der Typografie: www.tage-der-typografie.de

TDC (*Type Directors Club*): www.tdc.org

Tokyo TDC (*Tokyo Type Directors Club*): www.tdctokyo.org

Type Club of Toronto: www.typeclub.com

TypeCon: www.typecon.com

TYPO Berlin: www.typoberlin.de

Typografische Gesellschaft München: www.tgm-online.de

Typographic Circle: www.typocircle.co.uk

Typographische Gesellschaft Austria: www.typographischegesellschaft.at

The Typophiles: www.typophiles.com

Typotage Leipzig: www.typotage.de

TypoTechnica (Linotype): www.linotype.com/2084/fontevents.html

University of Macedonia Press: afroditi.uom.gr/uompress/enactivities.html

Western New York Book Arts Collaborative: wnybookarts.org

BLOGS AND FORUMS

2 ou 3 choses que je sais d'elle…: www.salutpublic.be/2ou3choses/

26 Symbols: www.26symbols.com

AisleOne: www.aisleone.net

All About Type: community.livejournal.com/ru_typography

Аматори Калізрафії (Calligraphy Club):
      community.livejournal.com/ua_calligraphy

Betatype: www.betatype.com

Daidala: www.daidala.com

Design et Typo: paris.blog.lemonde.fr

Ellen Lupton: Design Writing Research: www.elupton.com

The Font Feed: www.fontshop.com/fontfeed

Fontblog: www.fontblog.de

Fontshop Unzipped: www.fontshop.be

The Grid System: www.thegridsystem.org

I Love Typography: www.ilovetypography.com

Itchy Robot: www.itchyrobot.com

Letritas: www.letritas.blogspot.com

Lletraferits: lletraorama.blogspot.com

Opentype: www.opentype.info

Pentagram: blog.pentagram.com

Slanted Magazine: www.slanted.de

SpiekerBlog: www.spiekermann.com

TCL (*Tipografía.cl*): www.tipografia.cl

Textism: www.textism.com

This Day In Type: www.thisdayintype.com

Typblography: blogs.adobe.com/typblography

Type Desk: www.typedesk.com

Type For You: www.typeforyou.org

Type Forum: www.typeforum.de

TypeOff: www.typeoff.de

Typeradio: www.typeradio.org

Typies: typies.blogspot.com

TYPO.CZ: www.typo.cz

Typofilos: www.typomil.com/typofilos

Typografie.info: www.typografie.info

Le Typographe: www.typographe.com

Typographer: www.typographer.org

Typographica: www.typographica.org

Typographie/Un Cours À L'erg, Bruxelles: www.erg.be/blogs/huberlant

Типографія (Typography): community.livejournal.com/ua_typography

Typography needs you!: workshop.carvalho-bernau.com

Typoholic: www.typoholic.ru

Typomancy: www.typomancy.org

Typomilan: typomilan.blogspot.com

Typophile: www.typophile.com

Typorifik: frigorifik.blogspot.com

Index

THE TYPOGRAPHIC DESK REFERENCE

Designed by Theodore Rosendorf

Typeset in Decatur, Georgia

Edited and published in New Castle, Delaware

Printed and bound by Sheridan Books in Ann Arbor, Michigan

The principal text is set in Adobe Caslon, designed by Carol
Twombly in 1989. Adobe Caslon is based on original designs of
English typecutter William Caslon. The version used here has
been extended with additional custom glyphs.

Printed on Sheridan 55# House White

Bound in Arrestox Gunny Sak